To Hayden and Janet,
Congratulations on your
new purchase!
Love,
Juinta & Gary

JANET

The Restoration of a Victorian Yacht

Jonathan Watson

DAVID & CHARLES
Newton Abbot London North Pomfret (Vt)

British Library Cataloguing in Publication Data

Watson, Jonathan
    Janet: the restoration of a Victorian yacht.
    1. Janet (*Ship*)   2. Ships——Reconstruction
    3. Yachts and yachting——England
    I. Title
    623.8'223   VM331

ISBN 0-7153-8888-6

Phototypeset by ABM Typographics Limited, Hull
and printed in Great Britain
by Redwood Burn Ltd, Trowbridge, Wilts
for David & Charles Publishers plc
Brunel House   Newton Abbot   Devon

Published in the United States of America
by David & Charles Inc
North Pomfret   Vermont 05053   USA

CONTENTS

	Introduction	7
1	From Dream to Possession	9
2	Saving and Planning	17
3	Real Progress	28
4	Frustration	44
5	Gathering Way Again	52
6	Great Expectations	60
7	From a Tree to a Sail	65
8	Ever Onward	73
9	Old Gaffers Race 1984	86
10	Reflections	91

Appendices

1	Survey Notes	93
2	Hull Scantlings	104
3	Rigging Details	107
4	Tools	112
	Glossary of Terms	122
	Index	139

The joy of a job well done

INTRODUCTION

The stimulus to record the story of the rebuild of the *Janet* came from a desire to pass on my experience, my frustrations, and finally the immense satisfaction which resulted from not only the completion of the task but also every time I now sail her. I have tried to be as candid as possible by confessing my errors but at the same time putting emphasis on things which I feel are important. I hope that this record will act as a spur for someone who is aware of both the spiritual and financial burden an extensive rebuild of a vessel places upon its owner. Feel confident that with dedication, a colossal amount of labour, heartache and happiness such a rebuild will progress and the final goal achieved. The feeling is magnificent.

However, I hope also that this will deter the romantic, who only sees the wings of a gull on a balmy summer breeze, from embarking upon the same path. If he expects to complete the work in any sensible time by only putting in the odd weekend here and there and travelling fifty miles to and from the boat, then he is under the spell of his own delusion. I would suggest he leave the vessel for someone more suited to the task.

There is only one person who can decide whether the purchase is folly or not; he must follow his own heart, for deep down the true answer will be found.

It is worth bearing in mind that I work for a well-known ferry company and am granted regular and generous spells of leave. I am therefore aware how fortunate I am to have been able to devote a considerable amount of time to such a project. Without this sort of life style it would have taken very much longer than the two years which I spent rebuilding *Janet*.

J. A. Watson
Brightlingsea 1985

1
FROM DREAM TO POSSESSION

Around the country are the remains of vessels of many different origins, sizes and types, and since even some of the most decrepit wrecks have been restored, it is impossible to say precisely when a ship finally dies. This is the story of the discovery of one such hulk which was subsequently transported to what can only be described as a surburban garden behind a typical British 'semi' in Colchester and restored traditionally, using mainly hand tools, in keeping with the style of the period of her building.

This sad hulk, reflecting little of the purposeful beauty with which she was once endowed, was heaved ashore and abandoned in a lost corner of the Thames estuary. Left to endure this dismal fate, she was not quite forgotten and it was her advertised sale 'Morecambe Bay Prawner in need of restoration' which, by the slightest turn of fortune, led to my discovery of the *Janet* in 1978, lying in a boatyard on Canvey Island. As with many inshore working vessels, Morecambe Bay Prawners had evolved into very attractive, hardy boats well suited to their use and locality. It is not surprising, therefore, to find that with the rise in popularity of yachting during the latter part of the last century, the yachts, generally built in the same yards and by the same craftsmen, tended to be very similar in design to their working counterparts. It was clear that *Janet* had been built as a yacht faithfully on these lines.

Janet's length with counter would have been about 33ft since she drew 4ft 6in and had a beam of 8ft 6in, typical of her working counterpart. The latter were in fact open boats having a long narrow cockpit surrounded by low coamings and wide side

9

decks usually tongued and grooved rather than caulked. The fo'c's'le was the only protection from the weather and, even with the mast stepped well aft, provided only minimal storage and accommodation. The cutter rig was carried on a relatively short pole mast, and above the well-peaked mains'l the tops'l was carried on a yard. The long bowsprit ran outboard through a gammoning iron, and was normally set without a bobstay (Illus 1).

Janet was surrounded by an extraordinary collection of vessels in various stages of decay. Her decks were removed together with the beams and carlings. The inside of the hull had been completely stripped leaving neither beamshelf nor ties to hold her together (Illus 2).

It had already been discovered that, built by William Roberts of Chester in 1899, she was called the *Twll Du*, and later when she was registered at Liverpool in 1910 her name was changed to *Janet*. She was indeed a sorry sight. Vestiges of blue paint clung to her topsides and dried barnacles held a thick and

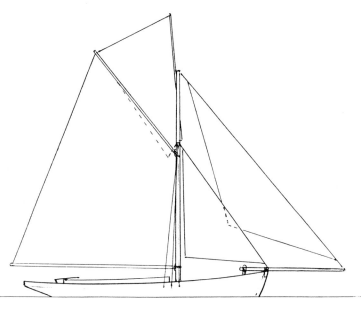

Illus 1 Sketch of working rig

Illus 2 First sighting of Janet

crumbling coat of tar on the bottom. The summer sun having free range to play on the unprotected inside of the hull had shrunk the planks away from the caulking leaving considerable gaps. My enthusiasm was not dulled by this sad apparition, but spurred on by the challenge I made a thorough survey of what was left, even though in my heart I already knew I would buy her. *

The iron keel, confirming that she had been built as a yacht not a working vessel, was on soft ground with only two shores each side which obviously did little more than prevent her toppling. Her counter had been sawn off and replaced by a mahogany transom. Even so the hull was definitely of Morecambe Bay origins, having the later form developed by Crosfield of Arnside and Armour at Fleetwood. The shape is classical with a cutaway stem, a rounded forefoot and spoonbow flowing into a curved

* See Appendix I.

11

keel and finishing at a steeply raking stern post, making the Prawners quick on the helm. The garboards are hollow, the bilges firm but well rounded, the midship section full, and the sheer line coming low down into what was once a rounded counter.

The majority of the yellow pine planking was in surprisingly good condition, even smelling of resin when scraped clean, but after seventy-nine years of use there were plenty of scars and graving pieces. Fortunately, though having been quarter sawn from the log, only very close grain had been presented to the outside, and consequently there had been no feathering or shaking of the pine. Originally expensive, this type of sawing of timber undoubtedly proved its worth (Illus 3). The copper clench fastenings holding the planks to the ribs were still malleable and not wasted; the quality of the copper used to make

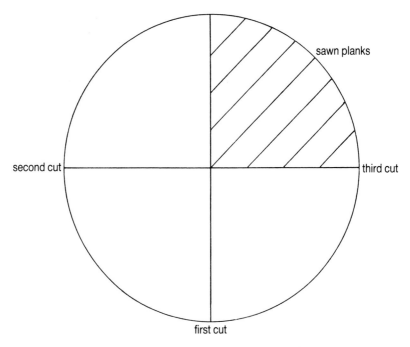

Illus 3 Diagram of quarter-sawn timber

these nails must have been very good. The iron fastenings, even though they had probably been wrought, had decayed virtually to dust, a process accelerated by being in contact with English oak. The acid content of oak, being fairly high, attacks ferrous metals quite fiercely. The steamed oak ribs were in reasonable shape at their lower ends, but about half had rotted from the top, clearly caused by leaking decks and fresh-water attack. The rotten ribs would of course require renewing.

The 'bones' – the sole piece or hog, stern post, stem and deadwoods – were all sound. In fact, being oak seasoned in salt water, these proved to be extremely hard and, as expected, held fastenings well. The top 18in of the stem was missing, leaving the top few plank ends jutting starkly; finding the missing piece later proved that it had suffered from rain-water attack. The garboards were elm and, having dried, had split for nearly their full length, but since half the ribs were to be replaced and the deadwoods thoroughly investigated they would have to be removed and renewed anyway. Her 1½ ton ballast keel was cast iron and showed no real sign of defect or decay, and undoubtedly it was this solid lump of iron which prevented the hull hogging. At the time of the survey I had not the where-withal to check the condition of the keel bolts but assumed that they would be badly wasted; a hunch which later proved one hundred per cent accurate!

Beside the *Janet* laid the remains of her deck and cabin top, together with a pile of rubbish which clearly belonged to her. In common with most traditional boat owners, I have a ten-dency towards kleptomania and consequently had a good rum-mage. My greed was well rewarded by finding a lovely teardrop deadlight, iron tiller and bronze gammoning iron, all three being part of her original gear and expensive to replace. A chap living aboard on a World War I steam pinnacle (unfortunately without engine or boiler) was happy to use the remainder of the pile of rubbish as winter fuel, much to the delight of the yard manager.

Although the shape, and the memory of what was once a proud little ship, was basically sound and rebuildable, the task was none the less daunting, particularly since her age and origin demanded proper and traditional restoration. Materials would be expensive, and possibly hard to locate. The amount of labour involved for one person was not to be underestimated. However, spurred on by the feeling that she was about the right size, was of known vintage and undoubtedly a thoroughbred, I found myself warming to her during the survey.

I took the plunge, arranged the purchase for £275 (about three and a half times her original building cost) and considered transport problems.

To ensure what I had just bought stayed as much in one piece, and in shape as far as possible, temporary beamshelves were bolted in, and beams nailed across them at about 3ft intervals. Shores were then wedged in between the beams and the hog. This arrangement would support the hull enough to withstand the compression of the lifting slings during craning and the bands holding it onto the transport vehicle (Illus 4).

A friend had just bought a transport business and was willing to move *Janet* for £50 from Canvey Island back to my house in Colchester. He agreed to back the trailer plus *Janet* down the driveway between a brick garage and the side of the house; not an easy task since the drive is 8ft 7in wide and the boat 8ft 6in. In theory at least, it was possible.

Janet was craned onto the trailer, lashed down and was at last under way. Under the weight, the back axle was hard against the suspension stops but the general feeling was that it was better that way than bouncing. I can still remember the great feeling of relief as we drove out of the yard. Up until then all plans and considerations were overshadowed by the onlooking crowd of sadly abandoned craft, some half-converted, some just falling apart, and others bearing no resemblance to sea-going vessels at all. Everything around seemed to be doomed to failure, so, from the moment of actual escape, there was a grand feeling of excitement.

I firmly believe that if a rebuild of a boat is undertaken then it is essential to position it as close to the back door of one's house as it is possible to arrange. The reason is simple. The jour-

14

Illus 4 Transport beams

ney from back door to boat will be travelled many thousands of times, but the journey from place of rebuild to sea only once. It also means that the telephone is close at hand, and working hours on the boat are not lost waiting for some supplier to call back. *Janet's* stem (when replaced) was finally some 12ft from the back door!

We arrived back at the house without mishap, and commenced the backing-in process. It took three hours but we made it, and at last after all the preparation, including moving the garage down the garden to act as a workshop and making room for *Janet* to stand on the base, she was there and the job could really start.

2
SAVING AND PLANNING

The first task was to clean every part both inside and outside the hull; scrape off all the paint, varnish and tar which for years had covered the timber and decide what required renewing, and what could be left. By carefully removing both garboards, access was gained to all the odd places which could not be examined properly before. As they came away the vast majority of the muck in the bilge came as well. All the lower ends of the ribs came to light, together with the deadwoods, and to my great relief I found no unexpected horrors. The deadwoods were sound. Incidentally, the copper clenches fastening the garboards to the ribs were cut at the face between the rib and inner garboard surface using a broken machine hacksaw blade sharpened to a chisel point, and used as a chisel. A reasonably heavy hammer was chosen, and the blows firm and precise. This way little or no damage was done to the timber, and the clench was cleanly cut.

Scraping the hull proved a much greater task than first met the eye. In all it took six days of filthy hard work. However, it was rewarding to see the tar and paint melt away under flame and blade leaving the clean resin-laden pine beneath. I was surprised at how little penetration into the timber had taken place other than places on the bottom, where the hot tar had actually darkened the colour of the timber to deep mahogany. After each day's scraping, warm linseed oil was applied to the freshly bared wood, which finally absorbed a total of seven gallons. I am convinced that the pine will now happily last for eternity! The oak, although dry, absorbed somewhat less than the pine, but still it was applied until it could take no more and just formed a skin. It was fascinating during this time to discover the

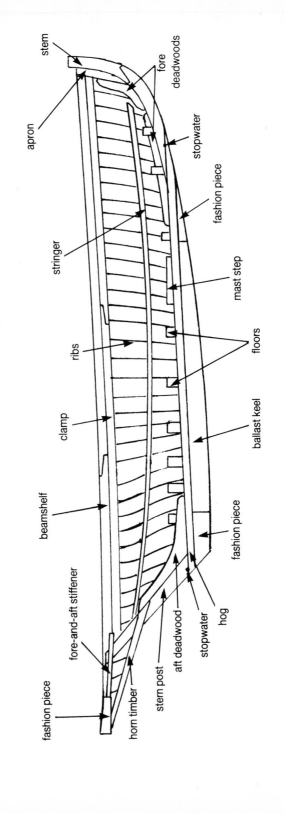

stem

fore

deadwoods

apron

stopwater

stringer

fashion piece

mast step

ribs

floors

clamp

beamshelf

ballast keel

fore-and-aft stiffener

fashion piece

fashion piece

horn timber

stern post

aft deadwood

stopwater

hog

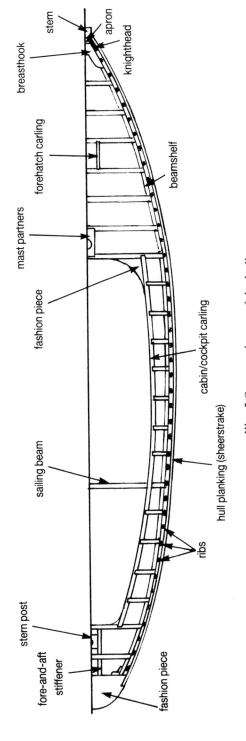

stem

apron

knighthead

breasthook

forehatch carling

beamshelf

mast partners

fashion piece

cabin/cockpit carling

sailing beam

hull planking (sheerstrake)

ribs

stern post

fore-and-aft stiffener

fashion piece

Illus 5 Structural parts of the hull

builder's pencil marks still sharp and clear after seventy-nine years. Even if Will Roberts expected his boat to last eight decades, he probably did not expect the pencil lining to do the same. Once all the timber had been exposed it could be seen that the original survey had fortunately proved largely correct. The main structure, planking and half the ribs were sound, iron fastenings would all need replacing, together with iron floors and keel bolts. There were odd patches of rot in the planks mainly at the aft end together with topside scars, the latter just requiring graving pieces. Around the bow, the four top plank ends each side, although not rotten, had lost most of their strength, owing to the weakness of the stem and fresh-water attack. It seemed unnecessary to renew these eight planks, particularly since finding 1⅛in planks 36ft long was difficult, and transport very expensive, but I was not prepared to have butts in the fore ends of the planks. When the time came to scarf in the top new section of the stem, it would be backed with an oversize apron, a further deadwood, and a good sized knee across the scarf. Knightheads were to be let into the deadwood and the plank ends then fastened into the knightheads. It is strange now to gaze at her graceful almost delicate bow and consider that it is virtually solid for about 14in at the forefoot. The sheerstrake was to be renewed. Even though a new piece had been tacked round, it appeared to be of dubious origin, and did not fit particularly well.

The restoration of the hull itself could not commence before creating a sound basis for the rebuilding. The old shipwright's adage 'it takes no time to rend out but many hours of patient labour to put back' came into its own. Oddly enough it took nearly a day of pondering to decide actually where to start: obviously ribs (Illus 5). The first real hurdle was reached, namely materials. The ribs were originally steamed and bent into place and were 1½in oak of good quality and straight grain. To find timber suitable is not easy; certainly not available at the local DIY shop or chandler's! However, there is a family firm of sawyers in Wix, Essex, which is not unused to supplying the needs of the boat-building fraternity. Thus, cap in hand and heart in mouth, I approached with my order. A couple of days later I was the proud owner of a best set of 1in by 1½in oak 'bean poles' ever seen.

Janet has 44 ribs each side, and finally, of the 88, 50 were replaced. The old rib was removed by splitting and driving out the old copper clench nails after the dowel over the head of the nail had been drilled away. This is essential since if the dowel is not removed and the nail and dowel are driven out together, the outer surface of the plank splits away. The new piece was put into the steamer for eighty minutes, heaved out, thrust into place as fast as possible, and clamped. Each of the fifteen planks was fastened to the frame with two copper clench nails, and the rib itself was fastened to the oak hog using a galvanised drive screw. Incidentally, the holding power of the drive screws in the oak was colossal. I bent one driving it home, even though I had first drilled the correct sized hole, and I was unable to remove it as it failed under the pure tension of my efforts to extract it. About one in five ribs broke on bending and had to be discarded, so the replacement of the fifty frames took some eighty hours of actual steaming, and consumed 30lb of copper nails at £2 per 1lb.

The steamer was made from the forward buoyancy tank from a Montagu Whaler with a steam spout welded onto the top. A rubber pipe of 4in internal diameter slipped over the spout provided the steam tube. The whole lot was lagged wih old quilts, and fired by a Calor gas boiling ring. The best head of steam ever produced was on an occasion when all the lagging caught fire, which, being occupied with the removal of the old rib, I did not notice for about twenty minutes. The next rib bent superbly.

The replacement of the ribs was a most tedious and time-consuming task. Although at the end of each day's work it was possible to see the new wood, there appeared to be no actual progress, and on occasions when there were more breakages than normal it was necessary to conquer the frustration involved. For some of the copper clench nails I was unable to hold the dolly and clench the end, so help was necessary.

Thoughts now strayed to garboards, but prior to their fitting the stopwaters were renewed. These are dowels set into a hole drilled across the mating faces of a scarf joint. The two stop-waters in question were those where the stem and after dead-woods meet the hog, the idea being that when wet the dowel will swell and prevent water seeping through the scarf into the bilge. Often a wood such as cedar is used which will swell sufficiently to be watertight but will not pry the joint apart. I had already ordered the timber for the garboards, and again I was in luck. Pascal's of Wix were sawing an elm tree to make a replacement docking belting for one of the British Rail Harwich Continent Ferries. I carried home two planks 22ft long, 14in wide and 2¼in thick. The thickness was necessary to fashion the hollow section garboards, a notable Prawner feature. These two planks are probably the most important on any wooden vessel, and are partly employed in transmitting the stresses in hull to keel, so a good fit and tight seams are essential. The elm boards were a lovely salmon pink and, for elm, a joy to work. They were freshly sawn and appeared pliable enough to spring into place cold. The garboard is not only a fairly complex shape but also has a hefty twist and bend, so fitting was tricky (Illus 6).

Although full of shakes, the original garboards had been removed in one piece, and could be used as patterns. This enabled the initial cutting to be quite rapid and gave a guide to the angles to which the edges should be set. Had the originals not been whole, templates would have been necessary, made from hardboard or thin plywood, the angles of the plank edges being taken directly from the boat. After the shape had been roughed out and the convex curve produced on the inside sur-face using adze and plane, the edges were gradually planed to size. Test fittings took place after every few strokes of the plane to ensure not too much material was removed. As expected the plank sprung into place cold even though the force required was quite heavy. During one of the fittings, a shore slipped allowing the garboard to spring out hurling a wedge like a trebuchet some 50yd into a neighbouring garden. I waited for the crash as it

Illus 6 Garboard ready to fit. Close examination reveals the detailed construction of the *Janet*: the sole piece or hog can be seen over its entire length and depth, with the ribs let into it; the stern post and aft deadwoods are visible behind the trailing fronds of the plant in the foreground.

passed through a greenhouse, which fortunately never came. I did not bother to retrieve the wedge. Once a good fit was obtained, the two garboards were soaked in linseed oil and fastened into place; copper clench into each rib, galvanised drive screw into the oak hog between each rib.

Sitting on the ground with my feet under the keel proved to be the most comfortable position to adze the external shape into each garboard. Being hollow or concave, the adze is the most sensible tool to use for such a task. A chisel and mallet, although a possibility, would become tedious and extremely time consuming, as would a round plane. To finish, however, such a plane was used to produce a perfectly smooth surface. One amusing incident comes to mind. During the winter I had befriended a robin which took great interest whenever I un-

covered the wood pile. However, while shaping the port garboard the little chap was unwittingly sitting on the toe of my
left boot!

While the cleaning of the hull and replacement of the defective ribs had been progressing, several scale drawings were
made, and the stages of the rebuild planned in detail. To this
end advice was sought from two highly respected craftsmen in
Brightlingsea: Cyril White and Jimmy Lawrence. Cyril White
hailed from the Morecambe area and had as a young man extensively repaired a Prawner. During his career he built some of the
most successful of the racing Folkboats and, a septuagenarian
now, and semi-retired, has become one of the more noted
characters of the Brightlingsea Waterfront. He was found on
the day in question caulking the bottom of a bawley on the
hard. His guidance was requested and, without ceasing work or
altering the rhythm of his mallet, he instructed me to come to
his boatyard on the following day. So, with nervous gratitude
my steps were retraced up the hard. The next morning I was
presented with a file containing the notes of the scantlings he
had prepared in readiness for building a 32ft Prawner. These
proved invaluable. He also suggested that the mast should be
stepped 12in forward of the usual position to allow more cabin
space and ease the tendency these vessels have for weather-
helm. By the time I left, the entire morning had flashed past.

I proceeded to the sail loft and James Lawrence, one of the
finest traditional sailmakers in the country, who had for the
most part of his working life been the skipper of Thames sailing
barges while still operating commercially. With the demise of
the barge trade he took his barge the *Marjorie* into the charter
business before coming ashore and starting his sail loft in
Brightlingsea. He is a good friend and his loft bustles with good
humour and industry making every visit there a pleasure.
Jimmy, although a traditionalist, is always looking to improve
existing sail plans and enthusiastically received the suggestion
that the mast should be moved forward. A good couple of hours
were spent sketching further lines on the drawings, experi-
menting with higher and lower peaks, the cut of the headsails

and the lengths of the spars. There was considerable discussion about materials, the amount of hand and machine work, and the weights of cloths to be used. The final design was based upon the premise of the new mast position, and relative to the working rig a shorter gaff and bowsprit by 2ft and 1ft respectively. The appearance was pleasing and as far as it is possible to tell from a drawing the balance correct. Although the length of the boom remained the same as on the working rig, some 22ft, the effect of having the mast forward brought the clew of the mains'l inboard. For a small crew, these factors would make for easier handling of the mains'l and reduce the size of the tops'l slightly. Another important factor was that *Janet* had been built as a yacht with lighter scantlings than a working vessel, therefore requiring a smaller sail area. However, the essential character of the Morecambe Bay Prawner rig had been preserved (Illus 7).

From the establishment of the mast position, the plan of the cockpit, cabin and forehatch fell naturally into place. To pre-

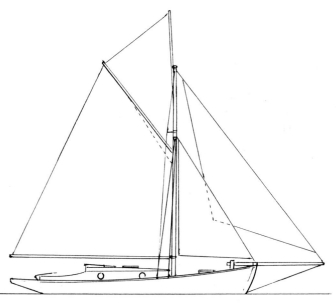

Illus 7 *Janet's* sail plan

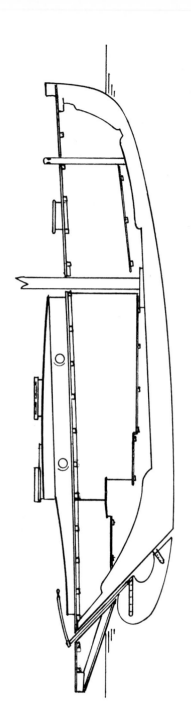
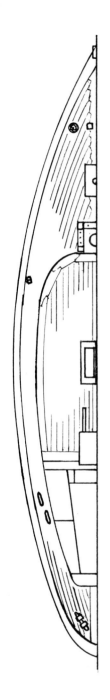

Illus 8 Sketch of plans – half-section through hull, and deck layout

serve the Victorian character the cabin was to have low sides, a pronounced camber and rounded front. The coach roof was to be planked, varnished and have a skylight in the middle. After several attempts and redraughts the most pleasing proportion was a cabin length of 11ft, leaving 7ft for the cockpit; the overall length being governed by mast and sternpost. The arrangement of deck beams, mast partners, carlings, the 'sailing beam', forehatch and samson post was drawn to scale and in detail to ensure smooth progress. The sailing beam incidentally is a full beam separating the cabin from the cockpit and greatly increases the support given to the midship section of the hull. From now on the stops were out and things went on at a grand rate. (Illus 5 and 8.)

3
REAL PROGRESS

To consolidate the hull had taken five months of constant work. The end of December was at hand, and winter well established. However, my spirits were high since at last it was possible to see progress being made. The stem was renewed as previously explained, and the sheerstrake also renewed to midships. Availability of timber resulted in the sheerstrake being fashioned of two lengths scarfed half-way, rather than the ideal single length. The after half of the sheerstrake ran through to the counter so the next logical step was to build the counter.

The hull section across the stern post was carefully bound in shape by using a strop and a spanish windlass was used to heave the planks in against a temporary plywood bulkhead just forward of the stern post. The old transom was removed by cutting each plank just forward of the inner transom surface. The truncated horn timbers had been led through the transom (exposing end grain to the elements incidentally) and firmly fastened to it. It proved to be quite a job disentangling the whole lot, but finally the transom fell away leaving a rather alarming breach in *Janet*'s tail end (Illus 9). At this point it was necessary to decide just how much to dismantle. The stumps of the old horn timbers were sound as were the stern post and cheeks. The cheeks were let into the horn timbers and securely bolted through the stern post and after fillet, forming the rudder stock trunking. To renew the horn timbers completely would mean dismantling the rudder trunking, at least two planks each side, all of which were sound. It was decided to scarf the new horn timbers on to the old. The addition of two fore-and-aft stiffeners under the deck beams level from the after end of the horn timbers to the top of the stern post would form a stout triangle and,

Illus 9 Transom cut away

all being oak and through-bolted, I considered this would provide a satisfactory foundation around which to construct the counter (Illus 5).

The horn timbers were fashioned, and scarfed into the old. Unsupported, the structure was surprisingly firm. It had already been decided not to renew each plank which ran into the counter for several reasons. First, had that been done there would have been virtually none of the original vessel left; secondly, expense; thirdly, there seemed no reason to discard thoroughly good timber; and fourthly, by careful staggering of the butts, no detriment to the fore-and-aft strength of the vessel would ensue. Four planks each side were run into the rabbet in the horn timbers. Throughout the rebuild Mr Clift of Clift Sawmills in Colchester was marvellous and came up with some top-notch larch for the planking. He was a kindly man who had been in the timber trade from the outset of his working life, since it was his grandfather who had started the firm in the middle of the last century on what was then the outskirts of the town. At present the sawmill has been surrounded by 130 years of urban development and is of course now quite close to the town centre. Mr Clift offered considerable advice as well as good timber at very generous rates and my gratitude to him is remembered every time I look closely at the quality of the wood put into *Janet*. However, I digress. The four planks brought the new wood up to the end of the horn timbers and to the start of the eliptical stern.

The size and depth of the end of the counter made framing impractical, and a solid fashion piece was used. Unfortunately, since oak of sufficient size was not available to make such a piece, hesitantly elm was substituted. Elm is very good under the water (particularly salt water) and will last for literally hundreds of years. However, where subject to wet and dry conditions, its longevity is suspect. The fashion piece was made from a piece 4in thick, 3ft long and 18in across. It proved to be a long job; the shape being quite complex to accommodate the joining of each plank, the turn of the planks into the sheerstrake and the actual shape of the stern itself. Finally, before fitting, coat after coat of raw linseed oil was applied until a skin formed, thus sealing the wood for, I hope, ever (Illus 10).

Once securely bolted onto the horn timbers, the remainder of the planks were butted, and run up to and fastened onto the fashion piece; one plank one side, and its opposite number the other side so as to balance the load. The bend and twist applied to each plank was at first somewhat alarming, but towards the end I became quite confident and heaved and pulled without fear. However, when fitting the third plank up on the port side there was a slight crack as the last spike was hammered home, but no shake or crack was visible. A week later the plank had split in half and had to be removed and replaced. The rest of the planks gave no trouble and sprang into place quite readily (Illus 11).

Illus 10 Horn timbers and fashion piece

Illus 11 Counter nearing completion

I made what appears in hindsight a very elementary mistake, which was due to lack of experience at the time. In section, the counter at its end is quite flat, and turns very sharply into the near vertical plane at its sides. Somehow I managed to fit narrow planks across the flat bottom, and wide planks on the turn. This led to planing the curve into the thickness of the plank resulting in rather more work than necessary, and more important a slight loss of strength. However, I considered this loss of strength was not sufficient to require undoing what I had built and starting again. This might prove a useful note for anyone commencing from the same level of experience as myself (Illus 12).

At last the counter was finished and the hull regained the natural grace and charm of the classic Morecambe Bay Prawner. Instead of being squat and foreshortened, the line ran gracefully from the stem, through the beam, and melted into the counter, giving a length of just over 33ft. My confidence had grown having overcome the hardest part of the rebuild. There was still a very long way to go, but the hull was complete and strong once more. Being mid-April 1979 I had the whole of the summer leaves to look forward to, and with luck might have her sailing in 1980. Looking at the hull from the ends showing off the new timber – stern, ribs, garboards, sheerstrake and complete counter – certainly boosted my enthusiasm. One small point worthy of note: the counter took 25lb of 2½in by 8 gauge copper nails at £2 per pound.

The hull was still held in shape by the temporary beams that had been installed to move the vessel, and it was necessary to remove these before proceeding with the deck. Without beams the structure would be unsupported and liable to twist or hog, therefore it was essential to shore up carefully under the turn of the bilges to ensure her shape was held true. The temporary beams were removed, and, by using a level and two plumb lines, an entire morning was spent alternately hardening and easing the shores setting the hull symmetrically about its centre axial plane. Finally, the top edge of the sheerstrake was planed to give the correct positive sheer, cocking up pertly into the counter.

Beamshelves were fitted – again larch from Mr Clift – 4in by 2in. They were sprung cold round the hull and bolted onto the top of every second frame scarfed amidships, since I was unable to obtain long enough timber to make one length. Later, after

Illus 12 The hull, cleaned and showing new counter, sheerstrake, garboard and stem. Close examination reveals new ribs and superficial defects on the planking, particularly at the stem rabbet.

the deck beams had been bolted on, a clamp which could be referred to as a second beamshelf was fitted under the beam-shelf, again scarfed amidships, well staggered from the beam-shelf scarf. This may have been erring towards belt and braces but when dealing with an ancient hull it is prudent to give it as much support as possible. Always with a rebuild of this kind there are likely to be inherent weaknesses which, with careful addition of new timber, may be overcome.

The breasthook now required some consideration. The angle between the sides of *Janet* at her stem is fairly acute, typical of a spoon bow; so a breasthook needed to be fabricated. I carefully chose a nice piece of seasoned oak 2in thick and morticed the two halves of the hook together. Fastening with copper nails and roves as well as gluing made a good strong job. I have little faith in glue alone (largely due to my own ineptitude), particu-larly in a place which is never to be seen again, so when the bow is shouldering away seas and the breasthook is taking its share of the load, I am secure in the knowledge that even though the glue may have let go, the fastenings will hold. The completed breasthook was fastened to the beamshelves, the first two timbers and of course the stem itself (Illus 13).

I had set the beamshelves at a height to allow the deck beams to be let into their top, 1in, and to ensure a decent fit a half dovetail was cut, the aft end being normal to the boat's fore-and-aft axis. By chance Mr Clift had several larch trees which had grown on a bank, and consequently had curved upwards to stand vertically. The bend in the trees matched exactly the deck camber, namely 5in over 8ft length. Larch is not as strong as oak, so instead of having a 3in by 3in section it was decided to have it 3in by 3½in deep to give the required strength. When the timber arrived cut roughly to shape, I was surprised just how well the grain ran from end to end of each piece. Start-ing from the bow, each beam was planed up, a bead put on each bottom corner, and bolted to the beamshelf. Seven full beams made up the foredeck with longitudinals to carry the deck plank ends, eight half beams let into carlings made the cabin and cockpit with a full 'sailing beam' between. Four full beams were

Illus 13 Apron, deadwoods and knightheads

to make the poop deck leading into the fashion piece. Good-sized beams at 18in centres, stout carlings and neat fittings started to push things into shape nicely (Illus 14). *Janet* was just beginning to acquire her former self-respect and dignity. The structure also stiffened up dramatically, again a huge boost to morale. May had arrived, the weather improved and the evenings were light, greatly increasing the length of useful day. The dear little Montagu Whaler, my first boat conversion, had sold, thus easing the financial burden. This speeded the work since I could (within reason!) buy whatever I needed without having to wait for the next pay cheque.

With mast partners and carlings in place together with the forehatch coaming, the covering boards were fitted. Timber, again from Mr Clift, was kapur, and the covering boards were cut from 10in wide boards, 1½in thick. After planing they were down to about 1¼in which set the thickness for the deck from the same material. Each covering board was cut to shape, scarfed to the next, fastened to the deck beams with 2½in deck spikes, and screwed with 2½in brass screws to the top edge of the sheerstrake. There was a considerable amount of work involved, and the kapur was very tough on the tools; at the end of every day, it was necessary to sharpen the power saw blade, and power plane blades, both fairly time consuming. Once done, the king plank was fitted down the foredeck centre in readiness for the swept deck planks to be joggled into it. Just by the nature of material the king plank was made from two pieces with a central seam. I was quite pleased with the end result, and feel that the two pieces look better than one. The deck planks could now be sprung into place, each being some 20ft long, 3in wide in the midship section, tapering to 1½in wide at the stem. The bend over the 20ft length was 18in at the mid-point and during the laying of the deck not one broke. Starting at the outside and using sash cramps over the covering board and plank, each one was bent into place and fastened down, two spikes into every beam through each plank, one plank at a time each side of the boat, again to balance the load. The arrangement of the butts was carefully planned, and each

Illus 14 Beams, carlings and covering boards

length was run from end to end of the boat before commencing with the next plank.

Laying the deck involved a lot of careful fitting. At the fore end the planks had to be joggled into the king plank over the longitudinal beam, and at the aft end into the covering board. However, as the days passed, the expanse of rich red deck planks grew and the skeletal appearance of bare deck beams

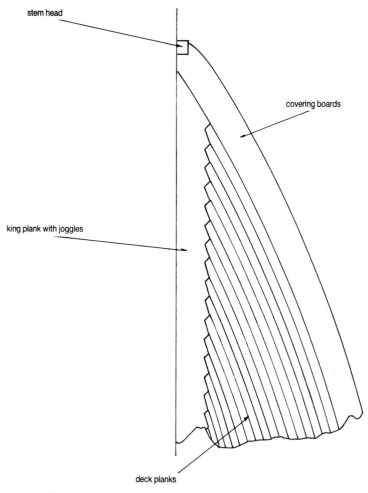

stem head

covering boards

king plank with joggles

deck planks

Illus 15 Detail of deck planks joggled into the king plank

38

vanished. (Illus 15.) By the end of July the deck was finally closed by the short planks either side of the mast. A hole was cut through the king plank and partners for the mast, and aft another hole allowed the rudder stock to come through the poop deck. The summer was galloping by, and since the deck had taken rather longer to lay than I had expected I was fearful I was going to miss another season's sailing. Having a full deck to walk on was gratifying though, and generally my spirits were high. It is worthy of note that a friend would kindly visit at weekends and, being a high-powered computer boffin, he was very pleased to occupy his mind and body quietly putting dowels into the fastening holes – a job I find more than tedious. He regarded it as 'occupational therapy'. (Illus 16 and 17.)

The time had come to plan in detail the cabin construction and to order material. I prayed the summer might continue into September so the major construction work could be done prior to the onset of the bad weather. The keel, rudder, cockpit, engine and other work could be done under cover.

All through August the weather was fairly kind, and progress on the cabin was steady. Enough iroko had been found to make the cockpit coamings and cabin sides in one length. Iroko is not the easiest of timbers to work, and tends to feather up when planed. The grain never seems to run the same way for more than 2in at a time. Two shaped sides were taken to a friend and put through his bench plane. An error was made when setting up and a hefty gouge was taken out of the end of one piece, leaving a scar *Janet* bears to this day (just one of the character bits). Fortunately it is on the inside of the cockpit and now, smoothed off and varnished, it is hardly noticeable. Once the sides were fitted, which proved fairly tricky getting the lie and the angles about right, they were bolted to the carlings. At this stage the tie bolts between the sheerstrake through the carling and cabin side were fitted. They were made of 3⁄8in brass rod threaded at each end.

I now questioned the wisdom of having a curved cabin front and curved corners to the cockpit, since the work involved in their fabrication was considerable. However, the rounded ends

Illus 16 Note the bend applied to deck planks

Illus 17 General deck progress

are essential to her Victorian flavour. By using 2in thick iroko, curved pieces were fashioned to make the corners, and one scarfed to the next and fastened in. By the time the cabin and cockpit sides and ends were completed, thirty-two pieces of wood had been fitted to make the round. As usual, when the job was complete the result was pleasing, therefore worth the extra time and effort. There is little wonder such labour-intensive craft are not built these days. The top edge was levelled and planed off all the way round ready for the coach roof covering board. I have a lovely old boxwood jack plane, which for this type of work is far easier to use and gives, I think, a better finish than a modern plane. Why, it is impossible to say, but through the entire rebuild the traditional tools always proved the more handy: the wooden-handle chisels, the boxwood planes and the trusty adze to name but a few. To be strictly fair, certainly the electric drill, plane and circular saw and later on the electric sander would have been sorely missed.

Larch was to be used for the beams for the coach roof, again because of the bent trees Mr Clift still had, and also because of the pleasing contrast between the light honey-coloured pine and rich red of the kapur boards. The size of the beams was 2in deep by 1½in wide and the camber at the aft end was 6in over 5ft. Having made a series of templates out of scrap timber, these were given to the sawmills and the beams cut to shape as had been the main deck beams. This saves hours of work as well as piles of timber, but a friendly sawmill is essential.

The beamshelf round the cabin side was 2in deep, and the beams half-jointed into it. The result was attractive and strong, and having a bead round the bottom of the beamshelf finished things off nicely. During the rebuilding of *Janet*, all the beams, beamshelves, carlings, deck planks, mast partners and coamings were all decorated with various sizes of bead to suit the size of wood. I had been lucky enough to buy a set of bead planes ranging from ⅛in to ¾in which had been advertised in the local newspaper; certainly, without these the below-decks work would have lacked finish.

Provision was made for the entrance hatch and skylight,

carlings and half-beams fitted in both cases. Once the covering boards had been fitted and the king plank was in place (incidentally, at the aft end, to accommodate the camber, the covering boards had to be steamed into place) the rest of the coach roof being merely fore and aft, planking was quite straightforward. The only complication was the fitting round the hatch and skylight openings.

It was well into September, but the weather was still fair; so on with caulking the coach roof and even some varnishing. The coach roof had seventeen coats of varnish all together, with only about the last five being neat. Four years on it is still good, and only needs a light sand and a couple of coats to cheer it up again. I am a great advocate of ordinary varnish done properly over a base of raw linseed oil which has had time to dry into the wood. I must have caught the caulking bug, since I continued and caulked and payed up the entire deck. It took five days of continuous work. Somehow the neighbours continued to be friendly even though the distinctive ring of the mallet on the iron echoed up and down the road from dawn 'til dusk.

My prayers had been answered, the weather had held long enough to make strident progress with the outside work, and the time had come to divert attentions to other parts of the task. Nearly twelve months' work lay ahead, but fresh life had been breathed into *Janet*. The winter was at hand and it was time to snug her down under the tarpaulin and tackle the engineering side of the task. One always feels one could have done more, but generally I was satisfied I had made the most of the summer.

4
FRUSTRATION

To make the best headway when the boat's restoration is completed outside, it is necessary to carefully divide the work into winter jobs and summer jobs. Further planning can provide wet-day summer jobs which can be turned to when the fickle English summer prevents deck laying etc. Skylights, doors, making knees, trips to chandlers, etc fall into this last category. However, the time had come to launch into my stock of winter work.

The interlude which followed will for ever stick in my mind as one of the most exasperating tasks during the entire project. Having already removed two of the keel bolts which came out fairly readily, seven remained (Illus 18). With the aid of a 3ft adjustable spanner, the tops of four bolts were wrung off. So using a whiff punch and maul an attempt was made to drive the remaining bolts out. After a full day of 'easing oil' and toil not one had budged. This actually may have riveted over the top end of the bolts within the hole, thereby compounding the problem. A jack hammer was hired and a special flat-ended bit prepared, but after a day of colossal noise that idea also proved fruitless. The next idea was to drill them out with the keel *in situ*, but the risk of damage to the hog was too great so the only recourse was to remove the keel. With the aid of a screw jack, blocks and levers, the 1.6 ton keel was removed and lowered onto 3in diameter rollers and rolled out from beneath the boat in true pyramid-building style, but with rather fewer slaves! The operation had taken another full day, making a total of four days without moving even one of the fast bolts. Using a ¾in electric drill, a pilot hole of ⅜in was drilled through each of the 15in long bolts in the mid-section of the keel, and the three

Illus 18 Sorry-looking keel bolts

12in bolts at the ends. The ratio of time spent drilling these holes to sharpening the drill was about 2 to 1 since the grind stone was a fairly diminutive affair. After two days the pilot holes were finished and at last some progress had been made.

The bolts were 1⅛in in diameter, quite manly to say the least, and with a brand new American drill bit some 9in long, welded to an extension shank, the main drilling commenced. I feel it suffices to say, after my own near despair, the keel ended up with seven 1⅛in holes and a drill bit 1⅛in in diameter and 3in long. The drilling took in total eight full days, starting at about 6.30 am and finishing at about 7.30 pm in the evening. I had tremendous moral support from my friend and entrepreneur John Grimwood who visited often, whisked me away for wonderful 'pie and chips' lunches, and basically kept me at it. Without his help, I think I would not have stuck it. I can still remember the immense relief when this particular job was completed.

The iron was given about six coats of warm tar varnish, the mating faces were cleaned and a gasket was made out of roofing felt. The keel was rolled back under the boat, smeared with 10 litres of 'black weatherguard' on the top surface, jacked into position and bolted home. Incidentally, the new bolts had been made by a friend in a shipyard, and cost 144 tea bags and a

Illus 19 Ballast keel after removal – note stubs of bolts which were subsequently drilled out

gallon of cooking oil: the barter system lives on! (Illus 19.)

The renewal of the keel bolts was not the only exasperating job that winter. An engine was a necessary appendage since the *Janet* was to fulfil the role of a family cruising yacht, and in these days of post moorings, marinas, crowded anchorages and deadline arrivals, it is not possible to depend one hundred per cent on the wind. One solution is to use an outboard engine, the advantages being ease of installation (merely the fabrication of a suitable bracket), cost and the lack of drag from a propeller when sailing. However, the convenience, reliability and the more seamanlike arrangement of a permanent installation were far more attractive. The Whaler, my previous boat, had been fitted with an outboard which had twice been swamped, and, since a wider cruising ground was hoped to be explored with the *Janet* than had been with the Whaler, the choice was easily made. From the outset of the project nothing less than a new engine had been considered but with dwindling resources a more realistic approach had to be made. Thus I purchased a second-hand 8hp Stuart with a 2:1 reduction gearbox, and stripped it down to the last nut with the intention of giving it a new lease of life; it had run acceptably for a second-hand engine so no real difficulty was foreseen. It was not apparent at the time but I had embarked upon a relationship with the wretched engine which was to try my patience as much as the removal of the keel bolts had done, and was to last for nearly a year.

A trip to Maldon with a list of spares required was made. The crankshaft and crankcase and covers were taken since special gear is required to deal with renewing the big-end bearings and reassembling the crankshaft; an unnecessary complication and certainly undesirable in a marine engine which may require maintenance or overhaul in the most obscure places with no more than basic hand tools. It transpired that the crankcase seals were obsolete and so an update kit was purchased. The magneto was tested – it seemed faultless, but a thing of very dubious design for marine use, with no waterproofing to any proper degree. Generally the condition of the engine was not bad, with all the castings sound and not turning to 'coal'. Everything was painstakingly cleaned and painted with Galvafroid as a primer and then two coats of green engine paint. Even the raised lettering had a coat of white to pick out the name as did the periphery of the fly wheel. New joints were fitted everywhere, new piston rings and bearings, new seals, and the carburettor overhauled and cleaned. Finally, reassembly was complete, and a test run took place on the workshop floor. After a modicum of coaxing the little engine spluttered into life, and, with a series of pails of water and odd hoses, a makeshift cooling system permitted a run of some thirty minutes. I stopped the engine and in keeping with good tradition had a beer.

The next few days were spent preparing the engine beds. They were made from oak, some 4in deep and 3in wide, and spanned between the aftermost floor to a very narrow floor straddling the after deadwood. A series of hardboard templates

47

were made to assist with their fitting which needs to be precise, since the load they carry is a compound of thrust, torque and vibration. The beds sloped, parallel with the axis of the existing propeller shaft, and of course required to be set at the correct height enabling the coupling on the engine gearbox to line up reasonably accurately with the coupling on the shaft. Needless to say, the progress was time consuming but finally the fore end of each bed was coach screwed into the main floor and the after end bolted through the wings of the narrow floor and the hull planking ensuring the firmest possible fastening.

The stern tube and shaft which had been *in situ* when *Janet* was purchased passed through the stern post and after dead-woods. Clearly by the proportion of the width of the stern post drilled away she had not been built with an engine in mind; the stern post was far too narrow. However, it was fairly thick fore and aft, and supported by the deadwood appeared not to have suffered. The caulking in the surrounding planking indicated that there had been no appreciable movement. By unscrewing the stuffing box from the inboard end of the tube and the two coach screws holding the shaft log onto the stern post the tube was slid out after the shaft had been drawn inboard. This was done prior to the fitting of the engine while free access to the inboard end was available. The tube fortunately came out quite readily, a fair indication of the dryness of the timber, and both it and the shaft were in good condition. The cutlass bearing in the shaft was barely worn, the shaft true and not grooved, and there was no sign of electrolytic corrosion on any of the surfaces.

After a liberal soaking with linseed oil inside the boring, bedding compound was applied (a mixture of white lead paste and putty), and the tube and shaft were replaced. When all was ready a friend came and helped with the engine installation. A pair of sheerlegs was erected alongside the boat made from two lengths of spare deck planking. A stake was firmly driven into the ground to act as an anchor point. A handy billy was slung from the apex of the sheerlegs, and two slings passed round the little engine. It was thus raised up and over the gunwale and cockpit coaming, and lowered onto the bed. The engine and gearbox were adjusted using shims to line up the gearbox coupling with the shaft coupling in all dimensional planes. The fuel tank was installed with deck-filler connection, vent to the deck, stopcock and feed to the engine. A copper exhaust was led from the engine to a through-hull fitting in the counter, well above the water-line. The water inlet via a Blake seacock was connected and discharged overboard and into the exhaust to cool and quieten the noise of escaping gases.

Using a garden hose as a cooling water supply, the engine was test run, and it was now the troubles began. The engine started easily and ran well for some five minutes when it stopped. All efforts to restart it failed, and on investigation it was found that the magneto drive was not turning. The engine was removed from the boat. To rectify the fault the engine had to be completely stripped, a distance piece put in to prevent the drive sprocket from moving and the engine reassembled. During this operation the crankshaft went out of line and when rebuilt the engine was 'stiff'. So, I had to strip it down again, and take the crankshaft to Maldon to be reset. Again it was rebuilt, test run on the workshop floor and reinstalled in the boat, again lining up the shaft and gearbox couplings. A short test run proved vaguely satisfactory so other work proceeded. This, however, was not the end of the battles with the fickle Stuart Turner.

With the engine and new keel bolts fitted there were several odd jobs craving attention, and although all of vital importance they had somehow been pushed to the bottom of the priority list. Still in the thick of winter, it was not possible to consider progressing with the main body of the outside work, so it proved a convenient time to clear these up.

The existing rudder was made from a plate of $^3/16$in or $^1/4$in steel, with angle iron stiffeners welded on to the sides. It was extremely heavy and was quite badly rusted in places, particularly around the propeller aperture. The new rudder was built of a series of planks placed edge to edge and bound with iron bands through bolted. The thickness at the leading edge was the same as the stern post, some $3^1/2$in and tapered to about $^3/4$in at the trailing edge. The extreme tip was virtually feathered, all of which contributed to a smooth flow of water past the hull and across the rudder surface. Unfortunately, having the shaft through the stern post, the rudder requires an aperture to make room for the propeller. This reduces the efficiency of the rudder and contributes to weather-helm. Erring on the side of caution, this aperture was made rather too large, and the clearance now existing between the rudder and propeller could have been reduced without fear of interference between the two. When motoring, the handling is very good of course, having the thrust from the propeller directly onto the rudder.

The rudder stock was made of iron, 1¼in in diameter and extended up through the rudder trunk with the iron tiller keyed onto it. The lower end had a ¼in by 1½in steel flat bar forged round and welded to it, so that the rudder lay between the two protruding horns formed by the strap. Bolts were used to fasten the rudder to the horns to facilitate removal if necessary. The lower end of the rudder hinges on a pintle fastened to the rudder in a similar manner as the stock, and locates in a bracket through bolted to the stern post. Necessarily very strong, the rudder can be subjected to considerable loads when sailing at speed and at times can be a vulnerable part of the vessel, particularly when taking the ground in a mud berth.

In the haste to advance, occasionally, instead of following a logical pattern, certain jobs were left to be completed at a later date. Morecambe Bay Prawners have a plank on the turn of the bilge which is thicker than the rest of the hull planks. *Janet* was no exception, and hers were made of oak. The starboard bilge plank had suffered fresh-water attack and had patches of rot. This had been removed very early in the restoration of the hull with the intent to replace it after the reframing was complete. It had been left until January 1980 before replacement. It is bad practice to leave jobs such as this, since if following a logical sequence there is a tendency to have the correct frame of mind and tools to hand, and generally speaking the jobs will be completed rather more quickly; things are never perfect.

Floors were the next step, and, although oak had been ordered, Mr Clift had the trunk of a sweet chestnut with a beautiful bend in it. Three 4in thick by 3ft 6in pieces were cut and shaped with the adze to fit the internal bilge profile. There was enough to put two additional floors in the bow. This gave a grand total of nine stout floors through the hull, seven of them being fastened to the sole piece or hog. The replacement of metal flat bar floors with solid timber spanning 3ft 6in athwart the hull will greatly have increased the overall strength of the vessel, and will tend to stop leaks starting along the garboard seam when sailing hard (Illus 5). Having the correct tool for the job made a huge difference to the shaping of the floors. Again second-hand, a most beautiful Sheffield forged-steel rip saw had been purchased for £10. The blade is some 3ft long and has the traditional cross-cut teeth, with a good set. Its own weight takes the saw through the wood, and all one needs to do is move it backwards and forwards and guide the cut.

To increase further the strength of the aged hull, a stringer was fitted to each side. They were arranged to run from the counter, about half-way between the horn timbers and the clamp, through the vessel about half-way between the sole piece and the turn of the bilge, and into the bow. They finished just short of the knightheads about half-way between the horns of the foremost floor and the clamp. The kapur planks used were 1in thick and 4in wide, and were bolted through the hull planks at every frame. Although their prime function is to lend support to the structure of the hull, they can be quite useful when installing the cabin furniture, by providing a convenient strong point from which to build up bunk fronts and the like.

5
GATHERING WAY AGAIN

It was pleasant to turn away from the series of engineering and oddment jobs which had occupied the last couple of months, since both the keel and engine work in particular had been somewhat fraught.

A problem which had been on my mind for some time was a supply of oak crooks from which to make knees. Only hanging knees would be necessary since the deck structure was solid enough. It is surprising how much work one can talk one's self around! No suitable timber had been available up to this time, when, on a visit to my parent's house near Titchfield, Hampshire, the question of oak crooks was raised. Having spoken to a local farmer, the result was a visit to a marsh, in fact the source of the old Hook River which once had its mouth at Warsash where Henry VIII moored his fleets. A lovely old oak tree had fallen in recent gales since the marsh had undermined its roots. It was one of the old English oaks, common in age of wooden ship building; a short but massive trunk giving way to enormous branches bending at right angles all the way to the last leaf on the twig. It was a remarkable piece of luck to have stumbled across enough knees to supply a first-rate ship of the line in Lord Nelson's Navy! It was with a certain amount of respect for the old tree that I cut the best boughs. I never cease to wonder at the majesty of a huge tree which has taken some hundreds of years to mature. However, part of that great tree will live on for as long as *Janet* survives. Enough of the crooks were taken to do the job together with a magnificent sweeping bend which has been used to continue the toe rail around the ellipse of the counter. From the crooks a set of grown knees was cut to tie the deck beams to the beamshelf and form a brace.

The end of February 1980 was at hand, and although there was a chink of light at the end of the tunnel a launch was still a long way off. On reflection it had seemed rather a slack winter, but being fortunate enough to have a whole month off I resolved to push ahead and not miss another season's sailing. Three planks of 1in oak had been seasoning in the loft for some twelve months, and it was from these that the forehatch, mainhatch and skylight were to be made. The two hatches were made in much the same way, planked fore and aft over a cambered frame. The joints and seams were glued and screwed making a firm job – necessary if leaks are not to occur. The forehatch had the teardrop deadlight let into its centre, allowing a glimmer of light into the fo'c's'le when the hatch is closed. The hatch was fitted by using a piano hinge on the fore side of the square coaming. The main hatch was arranged to slide on tapering coamings, being higher at the after end; quite an interesting fitting exercise to ensure the hatch was not a sloppy fit, but at the same time moved easily. When a hatch is arranged in this fashion, there is a danger of water being trapped between the runners on the coach roof. To combat this, holes were cut in the runners to let the water drain. Oak was used for

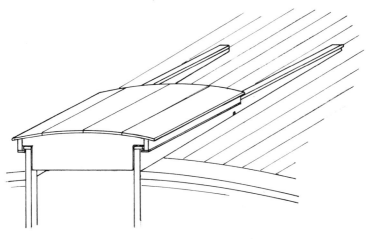

Illus 20 Detail of main hatch

53

the slides and provided a coat of beeswax is applied at the beginning of each season the hatch slides freely without binding. To complete the entrance hatch, two panelled doors were made, suitably beaded, and were fitted using 'lift off' or sliding butts to allow them to be completely removed when sailing (Illus 20).

On a craft the size of *Janet* I felt that it was not really necessary to have an opening skylight. The extra ventilation was not required, and it was considerably easier to make it fixed. The coamings were dovetailed into each other and fitted into the space in the centre of the coach roof. A proper arrangement of carling and half beams had been made to accommodate this coaming; again, an important feature if leaks are not to ensue later. A frame was made for each of the sloping sides, and $1/4$in plate glass was set into white lead and putty, finally being locked into place using beading. Again adequate drainage was provided to prevent water lying in the corners of the glass.

Prior to the fitting of the hatches and skylight they had all received coats of very thin varnish, ie about thirty per cent varnish and seventy per cent thinners. The dry oak drank coats of this mixture, and, finally topped off with a couple of coats of neat varnish, the natural beauty and figuring of the wood was brought out. Against the dark mahogany colour of the coach roof, the light oak made a very pleasing contrast, and certainly proved fussy enough to be Victorian.

Portholes were the next item on the agenda. I had decided after several fruitless attempts to purchase them new or second-hand, to make my own. Using sheet brass from a scrap merchant's, the round frames were turned on my ship's lathe. Since they were to be dead lights their construction was quite straightforward. The openings in the cabin sides should have been cut prior to their fitting, and, with the plank of iroko flat on a workbench, it would have been a simple matter of running round with a jig saw. However, with the lip of the coach roof and the main deck both preventing use of the jig saw, the four openings had to be cut with a key hole saw; a long and tedious task, and one for experience! Eventually the holes were cut and the brass surrounds were screwed to the side of the timber with the $1/4$in

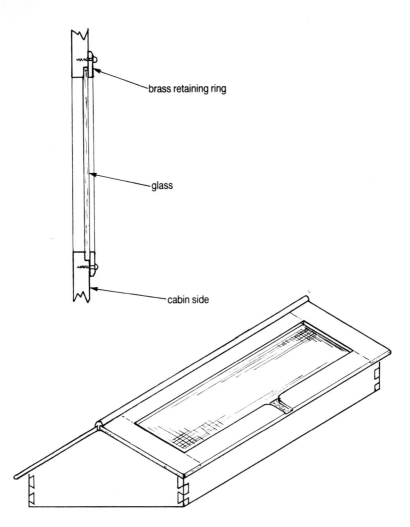

Illus 21 Detail of porthole and skylight

plate glass held firmly bedded in with putty, within a rabbet
(Illus 21).

᠄ I had mused for some time whether to cap the cockpit coaming, or leave the edge of the iroko merely rounded off. There
were some pieces of oak at hand suitable for the job, and two
small crooks from which bends to bring the capping round the
cockpit corners could be made. The time it would take to fit

55

these neatly round and finish by dowelling the screw counter bores was not to be underestimated. Finally this job was done and in hindsight the finish has certainly appeared far more professional.

To bring work up to date on deck, only the bitts remained to be fitted. Returning to the drawings to determine the distance from the stem, two neat square holes were cut through the foredeck, the foreside of the two holes in line with the after side of the deck beam. The oak posts were let through, scallops being cut in the corners to stop a rope slipping over the top. Below deck they were bolted to a single post, the heel of which was let into the hog. Each of the bitts was then bolted to the deck beam. The reason for the strength of the construction is that the compressive forces in the bowsprit due to the backward pull of bobstay, forestay and jib are all resolved into the hull via the bitts, and when sailing hard this must amount to several hundred pounds. Additionally, this is the stoutest mooring point or towing point on the vessel, both uses requiring considerable strength.

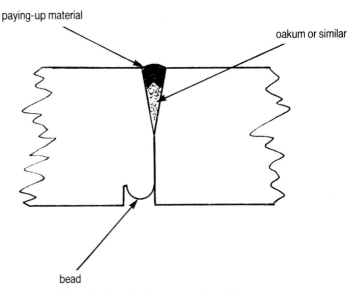

Illus 22 Sketch of a correctly caulked seam

There was still the mammoth task of caulking the entire hull. The only thing to do was to buckle down and get on with it. There is not a great amount of interesting discourse about caulking other than it should not be rushed, but done carefully and methodically, using the correct irons, mallet and materials. Gaskin was used for the threads since it is very similar to oakum and is used in the building trade for making joints in ceramic soil pipes; it is ready spun for use and treated so it is virtually rot-proof. Two threads of the gaskin were put into each seam, the total length of seam on *Janet*'s hull being 900ft. This made a total of 1800ft of caulking. Somehow, again, the long-suffering neighbours did not complain, and by the time the seams were caulked, primed with metallic pink primer, payed up wth a putty-red-lead-white-lead mixture and primed again, three weeks had elapsed (Illus 22).

It was now well into April of 1980, and although I had one more month's leave to come, the amount of work still left to do was quite alarming. By chance, a young lad who had recently left school and joined the ranks of the unemployed came to ask if he might help with some of the work. We agreed a rate of £25 per week (no questions asked) and I set him to work painting the hull. I was most grateful to this young boy since he primed, undercoated and painted the topsides, and put four or five coats of tar varnish on the bottom. He saved me hours of work and left me free to continue with the building tasks.

Henceforward the activity was feverish. All the surplus marine glue was scraped off the decks. The best time to attempt this task is very early in the morning, if possible when frosty, when the glue will break away quite readily. Fortunately the weather was kind and good, and advances were made.

The framing of the cockpit sole and lockers had already been put in. The sole was just plywood – a temporary arrangement, which lasted some three years! The locker tops were panelled using larch boards and plywood for the centre section, this method being reflected in the engine box lids. These two lids were an awkward job since it was necessary to make the lid over the gear box slightly lower than the lid over the engine to allow

Illus 23 A sunny evening, and the deck nearing completion

the gear handle to pass through. Again a messy piece of engine design. The lids doubled up as the step into the cabin but intruded into the cockpit considerably. These few jobs were quickly finished since by this time my rate of woodworking had increased considerably, particularly when using new materials and not trying to join up to old.

There were in stock some nice planks of 1½in oak which were fairly green and, being still quite pliable, they became the toe rail around the end of the deck. At the bow they were made 4in tall tapering down to 3in by the time they reached the chain plates and continuing on at that height. From the Hook River oak tree, the lovely sweep bend continued to the toe rail around the ellipse of the counter. Before having that bend the intention was just to taper the rail off to end just aft of the cockpit, but certainly the result would not have been as attractive as it is now.

The bronze gammoning iron was fitted on to the top of the stem, the naval pipe let into the foredeck, and the bronze fairleads let into the toe rail, two fore and two aft. The main deck was given coat after coat of linseed oil, and everything else was varnished.

On the poop deck two mooring cleats were fitted, made from the bronze hangers for a big ship alleyway hand rail, and two short pieces of oak let through – very Victorian.

The lad had finished the external hull painting, and also given the bilge a good few coats of tar varnish, and quite suddenly (or so it seemed) the time had come to move the old girl out of the garden. There were still several outstanding jobs to complete before the launch, but these were to be done on the quayside. My excitement at the prospect of launching her was immense (Illus 23).

6
GREAT EXPECTATIONS

It was a lovely feeling gazing at the sweep of the shining deck planks following the shape of the hull, each joggle neatly opposing its mate, all bounded by the oak toe rails curving evenly into the counter; the clean deep red of the varnished coach roof contrasted by the light oak bitts, forehatch, skylight and mainhatch, giving way to the varnished larch cockpit furniture. All of this was complemented by the cream topsides, and I am quite sure I spent at least an hour walking round, admiring her graceful lines. She certainly supports the adage of 'Not a straight plank in her'. This feeling of smug satisfaction soon disappeared when I realised it was the beginning of May, and there was still a long way to go before she could have a stitch of canvas set.

Peter Davies of Whippat Yacht Transport agreed to move *Janet* from the garden in Colchester down to the Hythe quay prior to the launch, or relaunch, since she had of course spent many years afloat before this time. He arrived at 7.30 am on 7 May. The way had been prepared by supporting the vessel on two legs so that the remaining shores could be removed and the trailer backed underneath. The trailer had a removable mid-section to allow the wheels and frame to pass either side of the keel blocks, then by raising the boat on jacks the blocks could be removed, the mid-section of the trailer replaced and the vessel lowered onto the trailer, the keel resting on the removable sections. It took from 7.30 am to about 10.00 am to back the empty trailer down the drive having about 3in clearance each side. We stopped for a 'cuppa', and secured the boat to the trailer. The old girl really was a tight fit being just 1in narrower than the narrowest part of the drive. We did give her a rub on the adjoining garage windowsill. Ironically this had happened on the way in, and instead of being white the face of the windowsill had spent the last twenty months a streaky shade of blue. However, on the outward journey this was changed to a streaky shade of cream!

The counter had been built over the garden shed and since there was not room to caulk the seams it had not been painted, so, most unbecoming to a Victorian lady, she had to travel some three miles with a little bare bottom presented for the world to see. Most improper! (Illus 24.) It was good to see her move, and certainly she left a huge hole in the garden.

The rest of the day was spent unloading and setting her up safely on the blocks on the quayside at the Hythe. At last it was possible to walk away from the boat and size her up from all ang-

Illus 24 Leaving the drive, 7 May 1980

les. Things appeared to be in proportion; at least the stern was straight and the counter in line.

First the counter was caulked, scrutinised by a little old chap who was almost a tramp but not quite. For the first hour it was rather unnerving but he said little and did not intrude. Only when the paying up was finished did he volunteer a remark: 'That own't leak', and disappeared. The counter was primed, undercoated and painted. At last the topsides were now the same colour all over.

There was a fashion piece to fit aft of the iron ballast keel under the sole piece or hog to fair the run of the keel into the rudder. The last remaining piece of sweet chestnut was used, and coach screwed into place. A good coat of antifouling was applied and every inch of the hull checked ready for the 'Great Day' – the launching.

Sunday 11 May 1980. This day dawned after a relatively sleepless night due to excessive excitement, and consequently I was up at the crack of dawn (quite unnecessarily) to check again that everything was ready. The star performer on this occasion was John Grimwood's magnificent old crane. It had been a field petrol tanker in the Libyan desert during World War II and was based on a Thornycroft Matador chassis. The tank had been removed and a 6 ton Coles crane had been put on. It had spent many years in the local scrapyard before being rescued by John G. We decided that it could cope with lifting *Janet* into the water and so we quietly waited for the tide to make enough to float her; it seemed to take an age. At last the time had come. John was his usual confident self, and his jovial face was a constant source of reassurance. The slings were passed around and carefully positioned, rags placed between them and the topsides to prevent marking and everything was checked again. It is peculiar how at events such as this a small crowd always gathers. That day was no exception. I gave John the signal to take the weight, and *Janet* lifted clear of the shores which all instantly fell over with a heartstopping crash. Gingerly she was swung round behind the crane. over the water and down to be returned to her natural element. It was with great

Illus 25 The launch – 11 May 1980

Illus 26 Afloat!

excitement that I watched the water creep up the keel, higher and higher until she was afloat. The bilge was checked to see if there was a mighty ingress of water. There was none; the odd slight seep here and there would take up as the wood became wet and swelled. Having spent twenty months walking on a perfectly firm deck, *Janet's* movement in the water caused me to stumble on more than one occasion, and to begin with the sensation was slightly unnerving.

The slings were slipped off and she was free. The rest of the afternoon was spent quietly consuming the greater part of a case of Heineken – merely to refresh the parts, you understand – and revelling in self-satisfaction. It had taken some 2,500 hours' work to reach this point and so I took the afternoon just to row around her and admire the beauty of the classic hull. I had of course painted in the water-line completely incorrectly – but who cared, she was afloat. (Illus 25 and 26.)

7
FROM A TREE TO A SAIL

A visit had been made some months previously to Dodnash Priory, Bentley, Suffolk, to select a tree from which to make the 33ft mast. It is best to choose a tree from the north side or middle of a forest since those on the south side tend to grow more quickly, therefore not quite so strong; also the heart tends not to be in the centre of the tree. This is owing to the trunk growing more quickly towards the warmth and light of the sun. A suitable Canadian spruce was found, large enough to be able to cut a 6in square section at the point where the hounds were to be. The tree was felled, and Peter Davies hauled it back to Colchester, where it was unloaded and set on blocks and trestles ready for squaring off. I enjoy making spars from trees using mainly an adze, followed by a boxwood jack plane. An electric plane obviously is used, but to finish, the boxwood plane leaves a smoother, cleaner surface.

When making a round spar, to obtain the correct diameters and tapers it is necessary to start by making the mast of square section over its whole length, the sides of the square being the same as the diameter of the finished circular section. This method ensures that the spar will be round and not oval, and straight with correct tapers – very difficult to achieve directly in the round. Considerable time and care was taken inspecting the tree to decide how best to hew the mast from it. It is important not to have any knots at the points of maximum load, such as at deck level and in the vicinity of the hounds. Careful marking is required to ensure that the first side is cut to the correct depth so that the centre of the tree will be in the centre of the finished spar, and the size of the square section is accurate over the whole length. To this end a string was stretched tightly between a nail at each end of the tree, to act as a straight edge, and a spirit level was used to ensure the face was flat and planar.

An adze is an extremely powerful tool, when used correctly and firmly, and if a razor-sharp cutting edge is maintained the side of a tree can be flattened out surprisingly quickly. By the evening the first side was flat and to size, and the second was half-way along. By midday on the third day's work, the mast was square and to size over its whole length. The bulk of the shaping was done, and to complete the round it was necessary merely to keep removing the corners systematically; eight to sixteen to thirty-two sides and so on. In the final stages the corners were planed off, and finished with sandpaper. Liberal coats of thinned raw linseed oil were applied finishing with copious coats of neat oil. The garden incidentally had turned into a sea of shavings.

Overall, *Janet's* mast is 33ft long, 6in diameter through the deck and up to the hounds, tapering down to 3½in at the top. The top mast band was actually only 3in diameter and butted up to a step. Above the mast band for the last 6in there is a sharp reducing taper, above which sits the button (or mast cap). The button plays an important part in that it prevents rain water attacking the end grain of the mast (Illus 27 and 28). Cheeks, trestle-trees, eye-bolts for the peak halyards, and a crane for the throat halyard were fitted in the appropriate places, and a tenon cut into the heel to fit into the mast step. The job took from Monday morning through to the following Saturday evening. To achieve this rate of work a concentrated effort had to be maintained. A slight transport problem arose since the mast needed to be moved to join the *Janet*. It was solved by removing the hitch from a dinghy trailer and lashing the mast on to the trailer with the axle just below the hounds, and using the hitch socket clamped to the heel of the mast. It was towed down to the Hythe behind the VW. It is probably illegal to tow a 33ft spar in this way, but we were lucky enough not to see a 'bobby' early on that Sunday morning.

There had been a trip to Daveys Ships Chandlers in the West Indian Dock Road, London to buy all those marvellous bits and

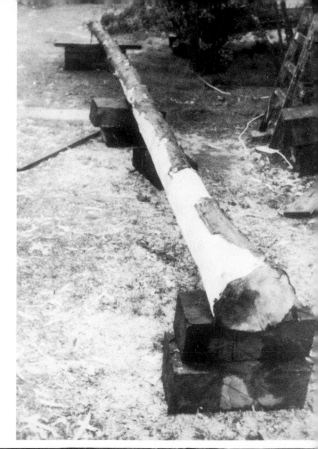

Illus 27 The mast from start . . .

Illus 28 . . . to finish

pieces which make a traditional vessel so attractive. I returned home some £200 poorer but with a car full of brass hinges and catches, brass lamps on gimbals, Norwegian wooden blocks, span shackles, twines, thimbles, hearts, needles and an elm-bottomed bucket in which to carry the smaller pieces. Although relatively expensive, it was very pleasant to see the gleaming new bronze alongside the deliciously smelling marline. It would not be long before great inroads were to be made into this bosun's store. Now that the mast was ready the standing rigging had to be made. The shrouds to the hounds were served, looped over the mast and seized to form a soft eye and two falls. The forestays both had a soft eye spliced into the top and served, as did the top shrouds (Illus 29).

Using the derrick from the 'crocus', a buoy tender, the mast was hoisted by hand in true Nelson style and lowered into place. Temporary wedges were set into the mast hole to hold it steady. The shrouds and stays were heaved up tight and seized to their respective rigging screws with bulldog grips. The inertia of the mast or masts on any sailing vessel has the same effect, acting much as an inverted pendulum and does not allow the hull to roll quickly. Proportions 'looked about right' for a Morecambe Bay Prawner, and the mast did not appear too mighty or cumbersome; if anything, slightly short but since the tops'l is rigged on a yard, a tall mainmast or top mast is not necessary. Once the length of each of the standing rigging wires was established, the mast was removed again, and the wires taken to Jimmy Lawrence to be 'Taluritted'. This was definitely a step away from tradition, but they are a neat fitting and I felt since I was having rigging screws and not dead eyes, a neat row of Talurits would not look out of place. Before the mast was stepped again, and the standing rigging set up, all the servings and seizings were given several good coats of Stockholm tar, which protects the materials from the ravages of time and weather. The old girl now really did start to take on her original appearance.

There had just arrived in the sail loft a new type of rope called Hempex. Although not cheap, it was a synthetic rope made to

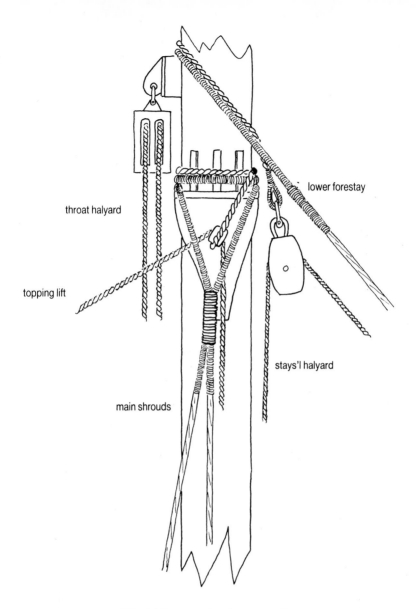

throat halyard

topping lift

main shrouds

lower forestay

stays'l halyard

Illus 29 Rigging details at hounds

look similar to untreated hemp. Ideal for traditional rigging, this was used to make all the halyards and sheets. The weather had been quite delightful, warm and sunny, perfect for making up all the running rigging. Gradually the seemingly endless splices, whippings and blocks became the running rigging and the mast appeared less naked then before. I greatly enjoyed this part of the job, since after the feverish activity and strenuous work it was most relaxing to sit in the May sunshine working with rope and twine. The odd trip aloft in the bosun's chair to bend each halyard as it was finished added to the pleasure of this task.

I had previously bought a log of lignum vitae from a chap who really did not know what it was or how to use it. From this six belaying pins – each 9in long and 1in diameter – were made and set into two oak fife rails either side of the mast. It is necessary not to underestimate the load on such rails from the combined tension of four halyards each 'swigged up' tight, so the supporting stanchions were made from 2in by 2in oak let through the deck and bolted to the deck beams below.

The bowsprit was made from a piece of larch, again from Mr Clift, who kindly cut it into a square leaving only the finishing to be done. I had the old mast traveller from the Whaler's sail rig and this (in RN style) was heavily galvanised and parcelled with leather – obviously an ideal bowsprit traveller. The two bitt posts were drilled together with the heel of the bowsprit, and once in place a brass pin was passed through and the bobstay heaved up tight. This arrangement allowed for the bowsprit to be retracted when moored or manoeuvring under power in close quarters, making things very much easier. It has the effect of reducing the boat's length from 42ft to 33ft (vital if ever a marina is to be visited for an overnight stay).

With the standing and running rigging complete, a long red pennant flying from the masthead and all the new varnish and paint gleaming in the June sunshine, together with polished bronze sheet cleats and gammoning iron, *Janet* had definitely regained her youth. The hull had settled down nicely, and the bilge was quite dry; actually spiders had taken up residence there which is always an encouraging sign!

Everything was ready, and she was waiting for the new suit of sails to come from Jimmy Lawrence in Brightlingsea. Work was progressing nicely on the mainsail for which she had to wait a further week or so. The problem with traditional sails is the amount of hand work which has to be done. This of course makes them expensive but I believe it is worth it in the long run. For the mainsail 8oz tan cotton had been chosen with hand-worked cringles, hemp bolt ropes and white stitching; for the staysail 6oz tan cotton similarly worked; for the large jib 8oz Berkmeisters white cotton. The natural white of the cotton and the dusky tan of the mainsail and staysail blended well together, the materials being the best Jimmy could find. The cost would be expensive compared with Terylene sails with little hand work, but the pleasure gained by handling and the lasting qualities of natural-fibre sails seem to have largely been forgotten. Providing they are dried carefully prior to winter storage and used or aired regularly during the season they will give many years of first-class service. The mainsail, staysail and large jib were the only sails which had been ordered, but these formed the basis of a comprehensive sail locker which was to accumulate over the subsequent few years.

I decided to return my attention to the engine. It did not run properly so out it came again and back to the workshop. There was nothing really wrong. The crankshaft went to the agents in Maldon yet again to be checked for alignment; it was dismantled and put together with 'loctite' in the hope that it would not move further. The guys in Maldon really were most helpful and seemed to put up with my seemingly endless visits with the resigned philosophy presumably gained only by years of patient work on Stuart Turner engines. The engine was rebuilt yet again and returned to *Janet*. It ran.

Jimmy had finished the mainsail, and a headsail was borrowed from Peter Powell (the assistant harbour master of Colchester Dock who at that time owned a gaff sloop which had been the sailing police boat on the River Colne in earlier years and named *Colne*). The day of the first sail had arrived, and an extract from *Janet's* log book sufficiently describes the day's events.

Voyage from – Colchester to Brightlingsea to Colchester – 6 July, 1980
H.W. Brightlingsea 0810 and 2030

		COURSE	WIND
0800	Cast off 'Crocus' Colchester	Var.	South Light/Var.
	Motored uneventfully down River Colne		
0830	Wivenhoe abeam – Engine running!	Var.	" " "
0910	Dropped anchor off Brightlingsea Hard. Harbour Master aboard for tea – served teas to all and sundry until 1410.		
1410	Bent on new mainsail		
1600	Up Anchor. Sailed out under borrowed headsail from Peter Powell and mainsail.	Var.	S3
1610	Boom crutch overboard – dropped anchor and retrieved it.		
1620	Made sail again.	Var.	S3
1720	Wivenhoe	Var.	S2 (Variable)
1800	Gybed several times to final reach of river	Var.	Light/Var.
1845	Moored to Crocus (No engine used)		

It had been a good day for the first sail, enough wind to sail, but gentle enough to iron out the first few wrinkles, and it left a very comfortable feeling deep down.

By the end of July 1980 Jimmy had finished the jib and staysail. Lignum vitae fairleads were set on the deck; and so, almost exactly two years from the day I had first set eyes on the sadly rotting hulk, *Janet* was restored and sailing.

8
EVER ONWARD

Janet was far from complete, even in the context that with a wooden boat 'things are never quite finished'. Below required totally fitting out and she had some rather nasty sailing habits, both of which took several seasons to sort out. Resolved not to lose a season's sailing it only left the winter months for general maintenance, and to continue with fitting the accommodation.

In 1981 *Janet* took aboard a proper mate. I was married, and Carol soon became absorbed by the continuing restoration of the old yacht. Somehow she always understood that 'back by about half past five', really meant not too long after eight o'clock!

One major change, however, took place immediately. As soon as *Janet* was laid up at the end of 1980 the dreadful Stuart Turner was removed. During that first short season it had caused endless headaches and worry. It tended to stop without warning in the most embarrassing situations, and was almost impossible to start when hot. On one occasion I was convinced there was a polythene bag around the propeller and beached the *Janet* for investigation. No bag was found, and on refloating, the engine ran normally! The final decision about its future came when off Felixstowe in light airs. It failed in the middle of the very busy deep water approach to the Docks and it was necessary to row the *Janet* clear of the shipping lane. From that moment on the *Janet* and the fickle engine were destined to part company.

In its place a twin cylinder 10hp Marstal engine was fitted. Made in Denmark the Marstal engine is a credit to its designers and builders. This was kindly donated by a family friend Jo Whines who was changing it for a larger engine in his own boat.

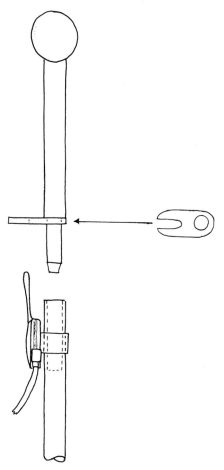

Illus 30 Sketch of gear lever and throttle arrangement

Rugged, tough, superbly crafted and finished, it felt like a
proper marine engine. Stripping, cleaning and valve-grinding
was all that was required. Pistons, rings, liners and bearings
were all first class and after painting it its original blue, it ran
beautifully. New engine beds were made since it sat much lower
than the Stuart Turner which had a 2:1 reduction. This of
course meant that the cockpit sole could be flush from end to
end, but for convenient access to the cabin a step cum engine
cover was fitted. This does allow a look at the engine while it is
running from the cockpit quite readily. The gear lever comes

through a removable short length plank in the sole, and is itself removable and incorporates a throttle. The gear lever extension fits into a socket on the top of the stub lever on to the side of which is clamped a Seagull outboard throttle control. The extension has two prongs on its side at the bottom end which locate either side of the throttle control when the extension is in place. Thus by twisting the extension the throttle control is moved. In practice, although sounding complicated it really is quite simple to install and use and has proved extremely handy for manoeuvring, since with one hand it is possible to engage the chosen gear and open or close the throttle simultaneously (Illus 30). The little Marstal engine has performed wonderfully and I fervently hope that it continues to do so!

Fitting out the accommodation was only commenced after precise planning. For a 33ft boat *Janet* has relatively little space below decks, an appreciable portion of her length being taken up by her counter and spoon bow. The side decks being 18in wide and the hull having low freeboard further restricted this usable space. However, the 8ft 6in beam together with cabin dimensions of 11ft by 5ft 6in did provide enough for a comfortable, if cosy, saloon (Illus 31).

Arranging the bunks with sitting head room under the side decks proved impossible, but they were set far enough out from the side of the hull to permit a comfortable sitting position with one's head inboard of the cabin side. It is necessary, however, to use a sail bag or large cushion as a back rest. They are both 6ft long, are set to the forward end of the cabin, and have storage lockers beneath. The bulkhead separating the main cabin from the fo'c's'le is staggered, allowing the port bunk to be set 18in further forward than the starboard. This arrangement allows for a larger doorway and more space for the galley which is at the after end of the cabin (Illus 32).

In the galley area a sink, sensible worktop and gimballed cooker were installed. The cooker has two rings, a grill and oven. Below the sink and worktop is a locker, cutlery drawer and day tank for the fresh-water supply to the sink. The locker front and doors are all made traditionally by setting a panel into

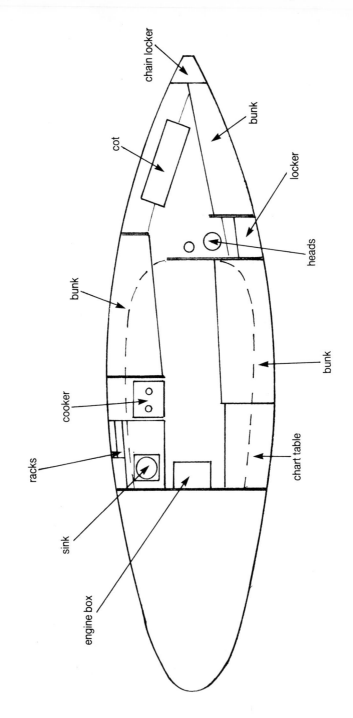

Illus 31 Accommodation arrangement

a teak frame; the frame being raised and profiled in keeping with Victorian style (Illus 33).

Behind the sink and worktop is a series of racks for plates, coffee, tea and other instantly required domestic items. The galley is separated from the port bunk by a half bulkhead in tongue-and-groove pine finished with a teak caprail, and on the inboard side a teak stanchion which extends vertically to the cabin deckhead.

Opposite the galley, the chart table and locker beneath were constructed in the same manner as the galley locker, and separated from the starboard bunk by a half bulkhead similar to that separating the galley and the port bunk. The chart table is large enough to accommodate a full-size Admiralty Chart laid flat, an important feature necessary to attain a reasonable standard of navigation. The locker contains a chart drawer where the charts can be stored, folded only at the printer's creases; the remaining locker space being used for general storage (Illus 34).

Below the entrance hatch the engine box doubles as a step and a seat for cooking or navigation. When not under way the chart table can be used as an extra galley worktop, greatly increasing the galley area.

The cabin arrangement has proved to be comfortable and the working areas simple and efficient in use. The panelling on the lockers and bunk fronts is of course varnished as are the pine tongue and groove bulkheads. Even with the deep mahogany of the sole and maroon mattress covers it is not dark and gloomy, since the skylight in the centre of the cabin top admits ample daylight which is reflected by the lightness of the pine bulkheads and cream paint on the inside of the hull. At night, by the light from the gimballed brass oil lamps, it becomes a cosy intimate saloon and with a heavy, sea-kindly hull and absence of aluminium spars aloft, it is only on the roughest of nights at anchor that one is ever disturbed. Embraced by the pleasant ambience of tradition and natural materials, I have found time spent below very restful and enjoyed sound repose. I much enjoyed fitting the cabin and giving time to curious little pieces of decoration. It is pleasant both aesthetically and in practice,

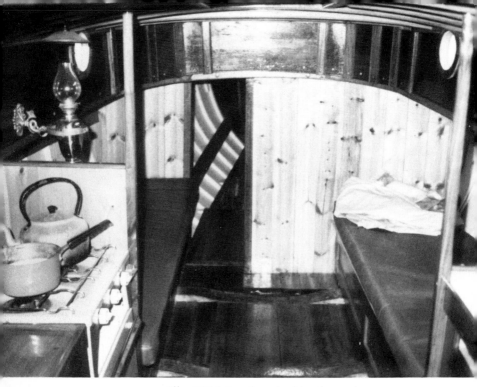

Illus 32 Main saloon looking forward

Illus 33 Main saloon looking aft: galley

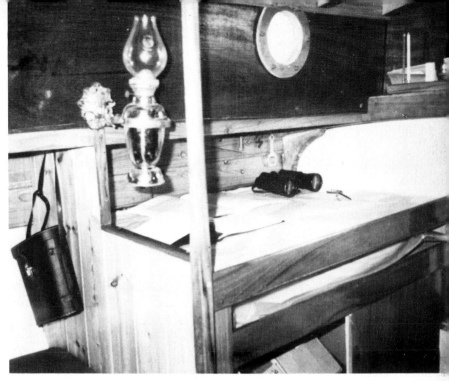

Illus 34 Main saloon looking aft: chart table

with of course apologies to anyone who has seen it and considers
it to be a mess!

A mistake which came to light in the first season was that the
main deck had been payed up with Jeffries marine glue. This
proved to be unsuitable. On such a small boat, the relative
movement between the deck planks and swelling and shrinking
of the timber itself extended beyond the elastic limit of the
fairly hard texture of the glue. It was raked out, the caulking
hardened up and the seams payed up with Jeffries Seamflex.
Being far more elastic this has virtually solved the problem of
deck leaks, particularly towards the end of the summer when
the timber has had several months to dry. Most important has
been to keep a good coating of linseed oil on the deck. This has
usually been done at the first opportunity after a week or so of
warm dry weather in the spring. The decks were scrubbed with
fresh water and soap powder, allowed to dry and given a liberal

coat. Another trick has been to varnish the underside of the deck planks which tends to seal the timber and maintain an even moisture content. On reflection the planks are really too wide, and would have been better at 2in at their widest point instead of 3in. Wooden oiled decks do require a considerable amount of attention but to canvas and paint them would take rather too much from *Janet*'s aesthetic appeal.

It has taken several seasons to learn how to sail the *Janet* properly and iron out the mistakes made with the rig. The most obvious fault when sailing was the considerable amount of weather-helm experienced when the wind strength was anything more than a slight breeze. The initial reaction was to reef the main, but this always stilted her performance and so it was not possible to obtain the best speed. I did of course fall into the trap of self-delusion, racing with much less powerful craft, or sailing off downwind and opening a gap between some other vessel heading vaguely in the same direction. It was not until the first entry into the East Coast Old Gaffers Race in 1982 that I really looked hard at my errors. I had made a fairly good start (about seventh or eighth over the line) and set off on the windward leg. After about four or five tacks, virtually the entire fleet had sailed past. Even looking for excuses, I had to admit the set of the rig was not quite as it should be.

Some friends had taken a photograph of us, and the first major error came to light. The jib was set too low, and the sheet far too far forward and near the centre line of the deck. This caused the clew to curl and backwind the stays'l. Secondly, I had not been peaking the mains'l up nearly far enough, causing the head of the sail to sag to leeward and the leech bag. The latter tends to move the centre of effort in the sail further aft which contributes to weather-helm. The luffs of the jib and stays'l were also sagging to leeward, indicating that the masthead was bending forward. I found this very saddening since I did not wish to fit running backstays. They can be dangerous (particularly Highfield levers) and are a nuisance for a husband-and-wife crew. It is something else to attend to when manoeuvring.

The first remedy was to move the lower shroud chain plates further aft, which I did through a distance of two ribs. Certainly this would contain the lower part of the mast. The cap shrouds were also led to the after chain plates which gave the top a slightly improved after support but still not sufficient. The real solution came from Jimmy Lawrence, the sailmaker; he suggested raising the peak halyard blocks further up the mast, and further out along the gaff. This balanced the fore-and-aft loads on the mast particularly when close-hauled. The tension in the mainsheet is transmitted through the sail to the gaff, to the peak halyard, to the mast all pulling down and back; then to the luffs of the jib and stays'l pulling down and forward and returned to the hull via the bowsprit and bobstay. The effect is remarkable, the luffs of the heads'ls can be swigged up nicely, and the tension between mainsheet and peak halyard prevents the mains'l peak sagging away to leeward.

The bad sheeting of the jib was solved by setting the sail on a strop at the tack, bodily raising the whole sail. This has allowed the sheet to be led further aft nearly to the widest part of the hull, thereby losing the curl at the clew and backwinding of the stays'l.

So far so good. The weather-helm had improved now that the two heads'ls worked efficiently together with the centre of effort further forward in the mains'l. The next weakness now showed. The bowsprit was made of larch, a very strong but extremely flexible timber. When the jib began to fill and draw, the bowsprit bent quite alarmingly, in fact when hit by a squall it once bent about twenty degrees and didn't snap. This tendency allowed the luff of the jib to slacken and the sail belly losing the forward drive. A new bowsprit was made from Douglas fir, a much stiffer, but heavier timber, and additionally it was made some 6in longer than the original to gain the greatest advantage over the weather-helm. It has proved to be excellent, enabling us to carry the large jib in a much stronger breeze, thereby holding on to a full main longer. The best known speed using full main, stays'l and large jib has been eight knots in still water on a reach over a measured mile. Still, though, she carried rather too much weather-helm, making an exhilarating day's sail fairly hard work for the helmsman.

The addition of a tops'l set on a 15ft yard changed *Janet's* light-weather performance from being a lumbering ox to a gazelle. Quite a dramatic statement, but this was how things felt. She bursts from bud to flower whenever the tops'l is set, and she will carry it up to about force 4 breeze on the Beaufort scale providing the sea is not too rough. The tops'l is made from cream Terylene, a deviation from traditional fibre, but since it has to be stowed rolled around its yard there is little chance of drying if stowed damp. Also, to do justice to the *Janet*, it ought to be made from Egyptian cotton which is far too expensive. After sailing with the tops'l set a few times, practice soon showed how best to set it. The sheet could easily be over-tightened losing all the shape in the sail, and hence efficiency. By just easing the tops'l sheet a fraction the jib and tops'l could be made to luff at the same time, a superb guide for keeping properly on the wind. The addition of the tops'l added to the relief of the weather-helm and *Janet* was becoming a real joy to sail.

To complete the sail locker a large lightweight genoa was made: 33ft 6in on the luff, 19ft in foot and 27ft on the leech; cut reasonably full for downwinding but flat enough for light-weather-windward work. This relatively monster sail is affectionately known as the 'Harry Driver', and that is just what it does! To avoid having runners and sliding fairleads on the deck (very non-traditional) to alter the set of the sail, the single whip sheet passes through a bull's-eye spliced into the end of a lizard, and depending on the point of sailing the lizard can be made off to the appropriate length through various scuppers in the toe rail. This incidentally is a very much cheaper arrangement than rails and travelling fairleads. Obviously with the Harry Driver and the stays'l set the weather-helm disappears altogether, but since the fore triangle is over-canvassed I consider that this is not a fair assessment of sailing trim.

The final adjustment which has solved weather-helm problems came not from the rig but from ballasting. *Janet* carries

Illus 35 *Janet* sailing with large jib

some half ton of pig iron as internal ballast, which gives her sufficient stiffness to stand to a breeze without fear of overpressing anything. The pigs were distributed evenly forward and after the heel of the mast. All of those forward of the mast were moved aft and packed tightly amidships. The effect is to relieve the downward force exerted by the leebow when heeling which tends to push the bow up to wind. The weather-helm is now cured, and it is possible by setting the sheets carefully for *Janet* happily to sail herself to windward with the tiller lashed; luffing gently in the puffs and paying off slightly in the lulls.

Downwind, with the Harry Driver boomed out and spilling into the jib and stays'l, and the mains'l and tops'l set with the

Illus 36 *Janet* sailing with Harry Driver

working jib set under the boom as a water sail, *Janet* flies six sails on one mast. The helmsman cannot possibly see where he is going, but the sight of her under this rig is quite impressive, and I use the maxim that all other vessels will be watching *Janet* and give her the right of way and plenty of sea room! From afar she appears as a faint echo from the days of the huge big class gaff cutters setting some 12,000 to 16,000sq ft of sail on one mast.

The tuning of the rig has been very much experimental, but finally without striving for too much perfection, *Janet* is now fairly well set up. I have learned a huge amount from her and I hope she is becoming a little accustomed to me. We do actually get along very well together.

In the five seasons sailing since the relaunch, *Janet* has cruised extensively in East Coast waters exploring rivers and creeks, and following Maurice Griffiths' wake through the swatchways discovering for herself their magic. She always attracts attention and many hundreds of photographs have been taken of her, particularly early in the season when her topsides sparkle with new cream paint and the varnish sports its rich shine (Illus 35 and 36).

9
OLD GAFFERS RACE, 1984

The race took place on Saturday 21 July and I was lucky enough to be home and get my entry off just in time. Friday was spent scrubbing out and storing up ready for the weekend and the arrival of my crew. Carol did not come since we considered the intensive day's sail to be too much for our ten month old daughter Thea and three and a half month old St Bernard puppy Baggy-wrinkle. Arthur Dobbs, an energetic pensioner, volunteered for the adventure having not sailed in this race before but quite an experienced race helmsman. We left on Friday evening at about 4.00 pm, motored clear of the Creek and set main, tops'l, Harry Driver and experimentally the large jib inside the Harry Driver. We romped up the Blackwater, with the dinghy fairly tugging at its painter, everything drawing on a nice reach. We resolved that this jib inside the Harry Driver was quite good and that we would use it come hell or high water on the morrow. We anchored off Stone Sailing Club, collected the sailing instructions, had supper and turned in for a pleasant night's sleep.

Although the start was not until 0830 we rose at about 0530, had a good breakfast and went on deck. There was a wonderful atmosphere of nervous anticipation in the air, and, aboard all the anchored yachts, smacks, bawleys, a Baltic trader and Dutch barge, there was a steady crescendo of activity. Looking around there were the familiar faces of the crew of the Harwich bawley *Helen and Violet*, and the Essex smack *ADC*. The *Jade*, an ex-Seaview Mermaid restored to gaff rig by Gayle Heard, swished past in business-like fashion in the light breeze showing off cheekily her immaculate white topsides.

Janet's engine was started. Arthur took the helm and the

anchor was heaved up – thankfully clean from the gravel bottom. We motored gently against the tide and came alongside the *Helen and Violet* to collect her dinghy and anchor it with ours in shallow water. It was fun to see the three lads from the sail loft, Mark, Ian and Sean, all highly skilled people, who would provide the brawn and muscle for the day. There was on board some 200 odd years of maritime experience in the guise of Cyril White, Jack Cook and of course the skipper Jimmy Lawrence. Jack Cook, like Cyril White, is well into his seventies, and started life at sea at the age of eight serving as a 'boy' on one of the huge professionally crewed yachts of the time. Racing some of the big class yachts between the wars, he assumed his own command in the 1930s and continued to serve the same owner until the mid 1970s. He has a marvellous sense of humour and of course many fascinating tales of real yachting. He is equally happy clearing a jammed topsail halyard sheeve as providing a perfectly fried egg from a spotless galley. Between the two boats excited wise cracks were passed, everyone laughing far too heartily at the silliest joke. Their dinghy was taken in tow, Arthur opened the throttle slightly, and bade good luck as *Janet* sheered away. Looking back we saw Mark and Sean swigging up the peak halyard waiting for Jimmy to give the signal to belay.

The wind was blowing lightly, straight down the River Blackwater and the ebb tide was running fairly swiftly – at least there was wind enough to sail but care must be taken not to be swept across the line too soon for there would be little chance of beating back. Careful attention was paid to the set of mains'l and Harry Driver – thank goodness the HD was cut flat enough to make good progress to windward. The spectacle was marvellous; a record entry of ninety-five vessels mostly sporting tan mains and stays'ls. The all-powerful rigs of the smacks and bawleys dominated the skyline, gracefully back-dropped by the finer more delicate rigs of the yachts. The age range was tremendous, with some of the older boats originally built in the 1870s (making us feel young at a vintage of 1899), through to some recently built ferro-concrete hulls – all wheeled sedately waiting for the starting gun. Three minutes to go, and we sighted the outer distance mark of the line. A quick discussion and round we went, booming out the Harry Driver. The large jib was run quickly inside it to catch the spill – it didn't fill so down to the deck again.

Glancing astern, I could see that we would make a reasonable start towards the head of the fleet, but since the shore line was completely blocked by acres of canvas I wondered if we would hold any kind of wind at all. The gun went and we were off, about forty-five seconds behind the line. The wind played all kinds of tricks for the next half hour, and the HD was gybed and the large jib was run up and down at least a dozen times. By the time we had the Power Station abeam, the wind had come slightly round to give us a broad reach. HD was gybed again and the jib run up; we hardened up the sheets slightly and made across to the windward side of the river as close to the mud as we dared, even though we were out of the main run of the tide. The wind held, and we found a fine gap opening up between us and the main body of the fleet astern. My excitement grew since at last we had a breeze in which we could sail the old girl. We held our position up to the first mark – the crack racers ahead of us of course, but none the less we were pleased with the progress. We even took a moment to brew a pot of tea! Very traditional.

Rounding the Knoll, the sheets were hardened and the water sail taken in as we came hard on the wind. The large jib was left inside the Harry Driver from the experience of the previous evening's sail. We held the starboard tack for about a cable and tacked. I omitted to pass the jib around the forestay so it acted like a brake for the entire tack, and since I was occupied with navigation to cheat the worst of the tide I did not notice until coming about for the next tack. On that tack we lost several places and of course time. The other error on this leg was, trying to make up for lost time, I laid off to tack into the main tideway gambling that it may have changed – it hadn't so it cost us more time – however, we were still well up with the fleet, and the long line of traditionally rigged vessels stretching way into the mouth of the Blackwater was a magnificent sight.

We rounded the North Buxey buoy and again came on to a

reach. The large jib did draw this time, and with the water sail we held off a smack from astern and made up another couple of positions.

By the time we had reached the Wallet Spitway buoy the wind had freshened to a nice 3 plus on the Beaufort scale, and the water sail was taken in. The stays'l was properly set in place of the jib. We had a dashing reach, everything drawing famously into the mouth of the river through far shallower water than I would choose to sail myself; however, we were on the heels of a smack obviously drawing more than us so we watched carefully for her to strike first. To keep a good note of our position I took eight fixes in three miles. We made up several positions – we were on our best point of sailing with an ideal breeze. Arthur reckoned we were doing eight knots at times; it certainly felt like it since the foam was fairly hissing past and *Janet* had a fine 'bone in her teeth'.

We came harder on the wind as we entered the river proper, and again although not in the best of the tide we hugged the windward shore. We held on to the HD even though in the odd puffs the bowsprit was bending considerably. Fortunately, having no sheet winches I could only swig it in hand-tight. This of course allowed Arthur, who was becoming more competitive by the minute, to spill wind from HD first and relieve the bowsprit load. Heaven knows what the old larch bowsprit would have done!

We drove on solidly, noticing that we were making up place after place as we held our windward position. I swigged in the tops'l sheet, halyard and downhaul and the main peak halyard, made sure the luffs of stays'l and HD were bar taut, anything to coax the last ounce of windward drive out of her. Resolved to hold the windward side, we then had a series of short tacks which involved running the Harry Driver sheet around the forestay and catching the sail in the eye of the wind; to miss the moment resulted in a hefty swigging in of the sheet, so the incentive was large to catch it correctly. It was after missing the eye of the wind that my hip flask came into play, it quickly revived the parts even 'Mavis Clark' doesn't know about. Still we made up several places and found ourselves very much among the leaders. We tacked for the last time well into the mouth of Bradwell Creek and hoped that we could lay the finishing line in one tack. This we did after painstaking trimming of the canvas once again, just pipping the smack the *Mary* who ran out of water and had to tack. It was a good feeling to hear the finishing klaxon, particularly after such a magnificent beat, and we both thought we had not done too badly.

We met the *Helen and Violet*'s lug-sailed dinghy, and thankfully collected our dinghy from them, anchored, signed the declaration, delivered it ashore and sank contentedly into a large foaming pint of beer, even though it was only about 1530. Shortly we discovered on corrected time we had finished fifth overall – not a prize-winner, but very satisfying.

If nothing else we proved that the large jib does not really work inside the Harry Driver.

10
REFLECTIONS

Many questions have been asked concerning the rebuild of the *Janet*, the most common being how the interest could be maintained for so long over one task. In fact, the rebuild was not solely one task but a series of many varying and distinctly separate parts, each one an entity and satisfying in itself. As a whole the rebuild was one hundred per cent absorbing, and other than continuing with a maritime career it was difficult to devote time willingly to anything else; however, such a frame of mind was probably necessary to achieve the goal in a reasonable time.

There is a critical time limit in the rebuild of an old vessel. If the time taken is too long then the new material which has been put into it will reach the stage where it will require maintaining or start to decay. Thus the time taken to carry out this maintenance will prevent advancement at the original rate and a vicious circle will be entered. A decision will have to be made as to whether to proceed and gradually become slower and slower, or to employ another or further persons to assist, which of course makes things very much more expensive.

This raises the question of cost. The cost of the rebuild of the *Janet* is unknown since no records were kept. As with everything it was probably more expensive than had been anticipated, but fortunately, by begging, borrowing and stealing as much as possible, keeping the weather eye open for bargains and never passing a second-hand chandler's, finances didn't actually stop the work although things did come pretty close at times. It is worth bearing in mind that at least a third of the total cost was consumed by the basic sails, mast and rigging. As with the construction work, never contemplate short cuts or half-hearted work aloft. When sailing, and the first unexpected squall strikes

91

the vessel, a flood of memories of odd bits which could have been done slightly better well up into poignant consciousness. However, if one has been strictly honest with oneself, done everything as reasonably well as possible, rest assured that boats are intrinsically very strong and will usually withstand far more than their owners.

On two occasions *Janet* has been pressed unexpectedly fairly hard and had water up to (but never over) the coamings. Thankfully, each time she has not carried away anything aloft, and subsequently not made any water. The arrangement of *Janet*'s machinery is not ideal. Petrol of course is very much more dangerous than diesel, since its vapour is heavier than air and can collect in the bilge. As with most things, the awareness of such a danger, the taking of diligent precautions to prevent any spillage or leak of petrol and the regular ventilation of the bilge will ensure the safety of the vessel and her crew.

The three-bladed propeller is situated in the rudder aperture, as already mentioned, and the handling under power is excellent. However, a two-bladed propeller would be better when sailing, since by marking the shaft inside the vessel the blades of the propeller could be lined up with the stern post, greatly reducing drag. The ideal solution is to have a wing engine with the shaft log mounted on the quarter and a feathering or folding propeller. Handling under power would not be quite so good since the thrust would not be directed on to the rudder. The two real advantages are the subsequent reduction in drag, particularly noticeable in light airs, and the absence of a relatively large hole bored through the stern post and the after dead-woods. It is unlikely that *Janet* will ever have a wing engine or feathering propeller, but hopefully a suitable two-bladed propeller will come to hand in the not too distant future.

Boats are very personal, and become more so when one devotes for a time the greater part of one's soul rescuing an old lady of the sea. The *Janet* is undoubtedly very close to my heart, and provides endless hours of pleasure to my family, relatives and friends, both distant and close. It is good to feel that after the effort which went into her restoration *Janet* is fun.

APPENDIX 1
SURVEY NOTES
(see illus 5)

These notes are pertinent to the survey of a yacht or working boat of length 20ft to 50ft. Although the same principles apply to the survey of larger vessels, their construction is more complex, and consequently the survey requires a higher level of expertise.

The decision to consider the purchase of a vessel usually satisfies the equation whose roots include the desires and intentions of the heart, the size of the purse and the range of vessels up for sale at the time. So, once this decision has been made, obviously a very close examination of the proposed acquisition must be made. Surveying yachts or small craft is a profession in itself and reputable surveyors are respected people; thoughts of conducting a survey oneself should not be taken lightly. To say the success or failure is dependent upon a correct and proper survey is somewhat dramatic, but if a major unexpected defect becomes apparent after the purchase has been made it is possible that the necessary repairs may prove beyond one's capabilities or facilities.

The first and most important factor is to be totally honest and objective. A professional surveyor will have no emotional involvement with what he is looking at, whereas for the prospective buyer the wish to complete the deal, taking on and completing any work, and the dreams of slipping the moorings on a fine summer's day is like 'the tempter' sitting on one's shoulder. Check back to one's own thoughts, and question the feeling that the boat really is what is wanted. Consider the size of the vessel. When ashore a boat can appear to be enormous, but afloat very much smaller. The intended use of the boat will play a very important role in the choice, as will the most frequented sailing grounds. To take extremes, it is a shame and waste to see a 70ft ketch used for picnics, and only ever sailing for a few hours each season; and, conversely, it would be unwise to have a 17ft day sailer if frequent trips across the North Sea are to be made.

It is necessary to decide whether a vessel is to be rebuilt, renovated, or whether the truth is merely to obtain a vessel in which to sail, being hopeful of a bargain. The latter is not for discussion here. There is a world of difference between a rebuild and a renovation, both in cost and the amount of labour, together with the type of work involved. A renovation will most probably consist of scraping back to bare timber, revarnishing and repainting, recaulking decks and hulls, attention to existing fittings and equipment coupled with odd repairs, possible recanvassing of decks or cabin tops, and finally an extensive fitting out. If it is a renovation which is proposed then the survey must be if anything more exact than if a rebuild is to be undertaken. The vessel in question will be in a reasonably serviceable condition and access to many areas will be restricted. Beware, a renovation may rapidly turn into a rebuild involving major structural work, and any doubts or any questions which cannot be readily answered with reasonable certainty must be fully researched.

A rebuild is of course precisely what the word describes. It is the dismantling of a vessel and replacement of each part as necessary with new timber, and often it can be more exacting than a new building. The amount of work and material should not be underestimated, and attention must be paid to the size and type of vessel under scrutiny. A 30ft yacht does not sound very much larger than a 25ft yacht. However, the volume increases by a factor of a cube of the length, and it is not unreasonable to assume that the amount of timber in a vessel increases at the same rate. An ex-working vessel will have heavier scantlings and require more timber than a like-sized yacht. Similarly the gear aloft will be heavier, larger and more expensive. It is worth bearing in mind that sails and rigging will make or break a successful rebuild and their cost increases dramatically with the increase of hull length. Finally, when considering a rebuild, the prospective owner must be confident of completing the task and aware of the enormous commitment involved. Nothing would be more disappointing than finding that the task proved too long or arduous to complete, and that the original enthusiasm wanes leaving an embarrassing white elephant.

If, and only if, the answer is 'yes all right' to every question which is inwardly asked, then proceed with the survey proper. Ask the vendor if you may have access to his vessel without his presence – it does make for better concentration. In any event warn him that a lengthy survey will ensue; at least a full day for a 30ft boat when a renovation is anticipated and probably more. If the boat is afloat it will need to be brought ashore. Inspection of the boat's gear can often take a day when laid up for the winter.

Try to obtain some sort of history of the vessel, and proceed with caution if there are 'hedgy' answers to questions. A wooden boat kept ashore too long will suffer. The planks will shrink and there will be a danger of subsequent over-caulking and bruised seams stimulating rot along the plank edges. Find out where and when the vessel was built. Trace the recent use the vessel has had. A well-used wooden boat will be in much better shape than one only sailed three times in a season. People who enjoy sailing frequently will tend to care for the boat, notice and attend to defects as they arise; the classic defect being a leaking deck, but more of that later. The first half hour of looking will soon show a general feeling of well-being or not.

Relax, slow down and enjoy the survey. It is the first real step towards the goal. Start by stepping well away from the vessel and run your eye from stem to stern and top to bottom of the entire hull. Assess the 'lie' of her. Jot all observations into a notebook. This applies equally to a hull which requires renovation or rebuilding. The sheer line should have an even run, not rising at the chain plates. Look for hogging which is extremely difficult to remedy even if the entire deck structure is removed. If a vessel is to be rebuilt, a slight hog is acceptable, providing it is very slight; generally, though, hogging indicates a collapsing structure. (Incidentally, hogging is usually found and is quite acceptable in the larger ex-working vessels.) Look for any sudden, hard angles; they will indicate damage beneath the planking to frames, ribs or to the 'bones', (ie hog, stem, stern post, etc).

A twist in the hull is probably less serious than a hog but may indicate weak fastenings or damage to the structure of the vessel. If a rebuild is anticipated then the causes can easily be found and remedied. However, if merely a renovation is expected, the causes of the twist must be located, and it may prove wise to seek the professional advice of surveyors or a boat builder. During a rebuild, though, after a twist has been rectified and the defective fastenings renewed, extra floors and substantial hanging knees to reinforce the structure should be fitted.

Before stepping aboard to make a detailed inspection consider the actual construction of the vessel. Imagine with 'X-ray sight' the stem and apron, keel, sole piece or hog, deadwoods, frames or ribs, beamshelves and deck beams. Try to obtain a mental picture of how they all fit together to form the structure of the boat. Imagine the points of stress: the area beneath the mast, around the stern post, in way of the chain plates, the forefoot, where the deck meets the cockpit or cabin coamings. These are all places where fastenings may be suspect, or water (particularly rain water) has lain and set up areas of decay. For a vessel which is to be renovated, firm taps with a plastic or hide mallet (of about 8oz) will show up trouble. A firm ringing 'clock' will indicate sound fastenings and timber, whereas a soggy muffled 'poff' will suggest concealed rot, or poor fastenings. Expect trouble in these areas when a vessel is to be rebuilt. Again, note any suspicions, and research them once aboard.

It is likely in an old boat that the plank to frame/rib fastenings are copper, and the larger fastenings used for stern post to sole piece or keel, the stem to keel, frames to keel, deadwood fastenings and the like will be wrought iron. Both for rebuild and renovation purposes suspect the iron fastenings. On drawing the odd few it may be possible to ascertain the remaining life left in the majority and when a renovation has been completed they may be replaced at a later date. Ballast keel bolts will either need drawing or checking with X-ray equipment. In the case of an intended rebuild, assume that all iron fastenings will need renewing as a matter of course. If any illusions exist in the mind about iron fastenings lasting for ever and a day, only suffering from surface pitting, refer back to Illus 18, 'sorry-looking keel bolts'. Bronze or copper fastenings will generally be good, but check the odd copper fastening for brittleness. Copper can work-harden and fail. Remember, the decay of fastenings is more often the reason that a vessel is hulked or discarded rather than rotten timber.

Go back to the mallet. Start the sounding at the stern post, along the planking over the horn timbers, then down the stern post to the garboard and follow the rabbet up to the stem. If the boat has a counter, pay special attention to the after hood ends where the internal ventilation is poor, and deck leaks will seldom have received attention. Similarly the fore hood ends will suffer from the same problem but probably not as severe as those in a counter stern. Again, record findings in a notebook and investigate further once aboard.

Carefully check the caulking along the garboard seam, around the stern post, and up the stem. It will indicate excessive relative movement, and the tell-tale signs that fastening trouble is present. If a vessel has been ashore for some time, it will have certainly 'opened up' a little and there may be shakes appearing in the stern post and stem, particularly if they are oak.

At last the time will have come to step aboard. Begin at the stem and work aft. Do not be satisfied with glossing over inaccessible areas behind cabin furniture. Get into cupboards and lockers and have a look and a smell. Use a mirror and torch to probe behind tanks (a favourite place for decay), sinks and the heads. Check every frame or rib from top to bottom. Probe down beside the apron, breasthook and deadwoods. Look for evidence of leaking decks, the greatest hazard for a wooden boat. Sea water generally does not rot timber, but tends to act as a preservative, almost 'pickling' the wood. Trees are designed to rot in the presence of damp musty conditions and return their nutrients to the earth. A deck leak will provide just this sort of damp musty condition in which rot thrives. The drip from a deck leak will find its way between the frames and planks, damaging the fastenings as well as the timber; it will lie in the bilge, under floors, penetrate between the garboard and keel or sole piece; it will lurk alongside deadwoods, under the hood ends between the apron and stem, and basically in any hidden crevice.

Smell will be the surest pointer to these kind of defects. A vessel which is cared for will be well ventilated, conscientiously covered in the winter or off-season months, and deck leaks prevented. These vessels will smell of tarred twine, linseed oil, paint and varnish reminiscent of a well-established chandler's store room. A pungent dank smell bringing to mind a crypt should sound warning bells. Obviously when considering a vessel for renovation or rebuild these sort of defects will be present but, if they are found and probed to their extent, when the work commences there will be no unexpected horrors to slow down the work or discourage the owner. It is in places such as these where trouble can exist and turn an anticipated renovation into a fairly extensive rebuild with all the incumbent consequences. Wooden boats advertise their defects, and will cry out to the surveyor: stains, lifting varnish or paint, smell, mildew or mould. Again, look at the points of stress: the mast partners, chain plate backing blocks, hanging or lodging knees, the corners of the cabin coamings or carlings, around floors and mast step or steps.

Proceed slowly, carefully and logically. A hacksaw blade ground to a blunt point will make a useful probe. Use it to scrape away dirt and 'potting compost' in the nooks and crannies and inspect the timber beneath. However an owner will rightfully take a dim view of knives and spikes driven into fairly reasonable paintwork, leaving a trail of damage. Refer to the notes made during the external examination relating to the position internally as each point is reached. Any defect seen externally (other than superficial scars) will become very apparent internally. Be quite sure the extent of any such damage or defect is fully explored before proceeding. Generally rot will tend to be found starting at the deck head, and working downwards; it will follow the 'flow' of rain water. Lower down, fastenings are likely to be the biggest headache. It is pointless to dwell on niceties. If the boat did not initially appear sufficiently attractive or suitable then a detailed survey would not have been undertaken. It is too easy to become carried away with the romantic notions of a prospective purchase. With old wooden boats, anything vaguely disagreeable found during the survey will instantly become a major problem once the purchase has been completed. Face the defect squarely, and record it faithfully in the notebook. Consider the remedial action necessary before proceeding to the next item.

There are many myths about why cement is found in the bottom of a boat. If it is found in a yacht, suspect what lies beneath. Generally it will have been put here to bodge up continual leaks from the garboard seams caused by weak or defective fastenings or to conceal unsightly wasted frame or rib ends. Very occasionally it will have been put in the bottom of ex-fishing boats between frames to give a smooth interior to the fish hold. It was usually cast on to a bed of tar, but even so the frames in contact with the concrete will most likely be rotten. If they are not it is a bonus, but certainly it would be wise to remove a small amount of the concrete to see what lies beneath. Clearly, if the purchase is not made then the damage must be made good at the expense of the declining purchaser. Assume the presence of cement will mean fairly major repair work is necessary.

Moving aft to the stern, odd items of little-used boat gear are often stored in a counter, again contributing to damp musty conditions. Look for mildew or mould on the deck head. Check where the frames meet the horn timbers and where the stern post passes through the hull. Search for rot around the internal framing or fashion piece at the extreme end. 'Sounding' of the after hood ends will have already given an idea of what is to be expected.

By now the notebook will contain a concise survey report and from it a reasonably accurate assessment of the condition of the hull may be made. It will also show up any areas of the hull that have not been scrutinised, and will be the time to take a breather and make a list of the repair work necessary to remedy all the defects which have been found. This will soon prove whether a renovation or rebuild is required and whether the prospective purchaser is prepared to take on the task. Now to proceed with the survey of any gear belonging to the vessel.

The boat's gear will be quite a good indication of how the boat has been used or abused. Natural-fibre sails will last longer if used than if left folded up without ever having an airing. If cared for, used and not left folded wet for weeks and weeks, modern proofed cotton sails will still be giving good service long after a Terylene sail has either decayed in ultra violet light from the sun, or chafed through all its stitching. Again, when looking at a sail, inspect the points of stress. The corners of the sail, throat, peak, clew, tack, head and reef points will soon reveal if a sail is serviceable or not. Rotten material is very easily spotted.

Expect wear or chafe in halyards and sheets. These are reasonably expendable and easy to replace. In the standing rigging, the lower ends which will have suffered salt-water attack will be where signs of weakness will show. Any patent terminal showing cracks or distortion will mean the shroud or stay will need to be renewed.

If the mast is stepped on the keel, and is still in the vessel, check very carefully its condition where it passes through the mast partners and underneath the mast gaiter. This is the most usual place for rot in the mast since rain water runs down shakes in the timber and gathers at this point; obviously since there is no ventilation rot will soon form. Tell-tale signs will be blackness or bursting of the surface. If in doubt have the mast lifted out of the boat. Any splice in the spar must be to a ratio of at least 12 to 1, ie for a 6in mast, the splice should be over 6ft. A glued joint will give no warning of failure, but will part suddenly; any 'lifting' at the extremities of a splice should be viewed with caution. There are, however, many yachts sailing perfectly well with spliced masts, and a spar which has been repaired professionally in a controlled atmosphere will give many years of good service.

For the rest of the gear aloft, common sense will be the best guide, but it is worthy of note that in the days of commercial sail, one-third of the entire cost of the vessel was reckoned to be spent above deck. Cracked or seized blocks will speak for themselves as will damaged or worn mast fittings.

In order to inspect the engine completely it will be necessary to remove it from the boat, strip it down, measure the wear on pistons, rings, cylinder liners, main bearing and crankpins on the crankshaft, inspect all the bearing shells, test the fuel valves (injectors) and fuel injection pump on manufacturer's test beds, or spark generation equipment in the case of a petrol engine. Clearly any owner would consider going to such lengths somewhat pedantic, particularly on a sailing vessel. A more practical solution is to run the engine under varying loads for a couple of hours and any major defect will generally show up. Check the engine restarts when hot. Check the oil before and after running. If it smells burnt there is a fair chance that the piston rings need replacing or the liners are worn. Excessive crankcase pressure giving rise to blue oil smoke in the engine compartment will point in the same direction; definitely piston rings will be defective and it would be reasonable to assume that cylinder liners will need replacement. Check the stern gland for leaks after the trip. The odd drip should cease when the engine is stopped or when an extra twist of grease is applied. A fast drip or trickle means at least the gland will need repacking or there is a worn bearing in the gearbox. In some cases the shaft may be scored or worn under the gland packing so if there are signs of excessive leakage the shaft should be removed for inspection.

Check that the engine beds are firm and there is no sign of movement between them, the engine or the hull.

Raw-water-cooled engines do have a life since the sea water will gradually attack the cast iron. Signs of the imminent demise of an engine owing to corroded castings will be runs of rust from fittings such as drain cocks or core plugs. Gently tap the sides of the block with a light hammer. A solid click will indicate sound casting whereas a hollow tinny sound will show the walls are fairly thin. Open the drain cocks and see if water runs. If it runs clear this shows the engine has been drained regularly and the waterways will be clear. A black slime exuding will point to corroded cast iron, and if it is impossible to clear the cocks with wire then the waterways will be fairly choked, and possible hot spots may have occurred in the cylinder walls. This may have caused very rapid wear in the least case, or seizure of the piston within the bore in the worst case.

Electrical systems connected with the engine, starters, dynamos, alternators and the like should be checked and proved to be working satisfactorily. Other than a strip down, inspection and insulation tests with a 'Megga', there is little more one can expect to do. This sort of equipment will always require a considerable amount of maintenance when subjected to life aboard a small yacht. Sea water and electrical equipment never make good bedfellows.

If there is not one, make an inventory of all the gear which belongs with the boat. A full inventory will often mean the boat has been used frequently and has been cared for. Conversely, with a boat which on paper has a good list of extra equipment which cannot subsequently be found, it is not unreasonable to assume that the boat has been left languishing for months at a time unattended – quite a good guide to the overall 'feel' of the boat. Jot down what is missing, or in the case of a small inventory what ought to be there, and make a quick assessment of the cost to provide the gear required. It will be quite a considerable sum.

The notebook will now contain a great deal of information about the boat you hope to 'wed'. Go away from the boat and read from the notebook every detail which has been recorded. Assess the amount of work necessary to render her seaworthy and sleep on it. Return a few days later quietly and alone, row round her if afloat, or walk round if ashore. This will be the time to decide whether she is to be bought or not. If she is purchased, the little notebook will be as important to the renovation or rebuild as a chart is to an ocean voyage.

APPENDIX 2
HULL SCANTLINGS

The scantlings listed below are the sizes of the individual structural parts of the *Janet*. As previously mentioned, advice was sought from Mr T. C. White of Brightlingsea who most generously made available to me a considerable amount of information concerning Morecambe Bay Prawners in general. Illus 5 and 37.

Janet	Morecambe Bay Prawner
Builder	Wm Roberts & Sons, Chester
Built	1899
Registered	Ex *Twll Du, Janet*, Liverpool 1910
Off. No	128036
Iron keel	Moulded – extreme dimensions 12ft × 15in × 12in
	volume 7.5ft^3 – weight 1.6 tons
Wood keel	Oak moulded – extreme dimensions 21ft of
(or sole)	6in × 16in × 6in
Floors	Sweet chestnut – 4in max span 36in, 6 at 24in centres
Stem	Oak moulded – 4in × 4in faired to oak keel
Stern post	Oak moulded – 4in × 5in let into oak keel
Deadwoods	Oak moulded – 4in at stern, 4in at bow
Horn timbers	Oak moulded – 3in × 3in – horn chock 4in × 4in
Knees	Oak moulded – 12 grown 2in
Planking	Canadian yellow pine – 1⅛in thick
Bilge plank	Oak moulded – 1½in thick
Ribs	Oak steamed – 44 each side, 1½in × 1⅛in, 9in centres

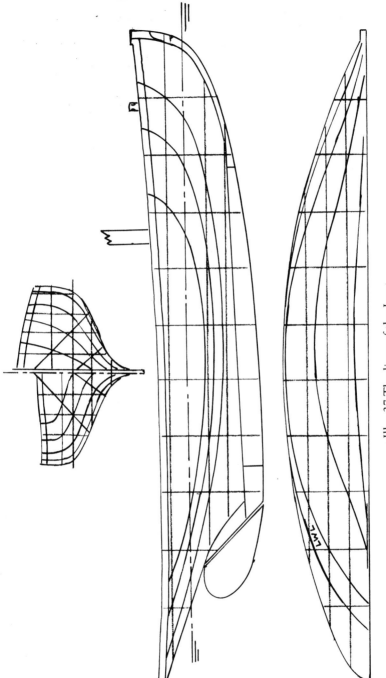

Illus 37 The lines of the *Janet*

Hull Scantlings

Beams	Larch grown – 10 full, 10 half, 3in × 3½in, 18in centres, 6in camber
Beamshelf	Larch – 6in × 2in
Clamp	Larch – 4in × 1½in
Carlings	Larch – 3½in × 1½in
Deck planks	Kapur – 3in max × 1¼in sprung
Covering boards	Kapur – 6in max × 1¼in moulded
Coamings	Iroko – 9in × 1in cornices fabricated
Cabin beams	Larch grown – 2in × 2in, 7 full, 2 half, camber 6in over 5ft
Cabin top	Kapur – 3in max × 1in straight
Hatches and skylight	Oak – 1in thick
Internal ballast	½ ton pig iron

RIGGING DETAILS

SPARS

Mast

| Canadian spruce | Length | 33ft – 4ft 6in below deck. 18ft to hounds. 10ft 6in hounds to truck. |
| | Diameter | 6in at deck. 6in at hounds. 3½in at truck. |

Boom

Norwegian spruce	Length	22ft
	Diameter	4in
	Jaws	Grown oak, through fastened and leather bound

Gaff

Norwegian spruce	Length	15ft
	Diameter	3in
	Jaws	Wrought-iron saddle, leather bound, fitted to steel cheeks fastened through.

Bowsprit

| Douglas fir | Length | 14ft 6in   10ft outboard |
| | Diameter | 4in 8 sided inside gammoning iron. Can be drawn inboard by removal of brass fid at bitts. |

Tops'l yard

| Aluminium | Length | 15ft |
| | Diameter | 2in, hollow extrusion. Ends plugged with wooden plugs rounded off. Painted cream. |

STANDING RIGGING

Shrouds

Galvanised standing rigging wire (plough steel). 8mm diameter. There are two shrouds each side of the mast. Each pair of shrouds is made from a single length of wire with thimbles at each end held in place by a Talurit splice. The wire was passed round the mast and the falls seized together to form a loop. The centre part of the wire forming the loop was wormed, parcelled and served prior to the seizing and given a good coat of Stockholm tar.

$\frac{3}{8}$in bottle screws were used at the lower ends for tensioning, which were in turn fastened to 20in chain plates.

Cap shrouds

6mm. Galvanised standing rigging wire (plough steel). One each side; each made from single length. Thimbles at the lower ends held similarly to those in the main shrouds. Passing through galvanised spreaders clamped round the mast above the hounds, the shrouds are finished by an eye splice, wormed, parcelled and served, looped over the top of the mast. The loop similarly treated with Stockholm tar. Again $\frac{3}{8}$in bottle screws were used.

Forestay

8mm. Galvanised standing rigging wire. Made up in the same manner as the cap shrouds and, using $\frac{3}{8}$in bottle screw, fastened at the lower end to the head of the gammoning iron.

Top forestay

6mm. Galvanised standing rigging wire. Made up in the same manner as the cap shrouds, and run from the truck to the krantz iron on the bowsprit end.

As mentioned in the text, the main shrouds were led well aft of the mast providing enough support without recourse to running backstays.

RUNNING RIGGING

Peak halyard 12mm Hempex
Made fast to the outer end of the gaff by a thimble spliced into
the halyard and shackled to a strop round the gaff, it was led
through a block on the mast, back to a block on a span (the span
and strop were made from 12mm pre-stretched Terylene) on
the gaff, through a block lower down the mast and to the deck.
This gives a 3 to 1 purchase. It is more usual, however, to start
the lead from the spar and then to the mast, to a block on the
outer end of the gaff and to the upper mast block and to the
deck, which gives a better pull on the gaff.

Throat halyard 12mm Hempex
The throat halyard was essentially a 3 to 1 purchase tackle made
fast to the throat eye in the mast just above the hounds. Its
lower end was made fast to the inboard end of the gaff on to a
plate. The plate allows the gaff to tilt but prevents it from
twisting.

Main sheet 14mm Hempex
The main sheet was set up to be double ended having a fall
made fast to a cleat on the deck either side of the tiller. From a
cleat the sheet was led through a single block on the deck to one
side of a double block on the boom, through a second single
block on the deck through the other side of the double on the
boom and to the opposite cleat, passing through a third single
block on the deck. This arrangement gave a 3 to 1 purchase.

Topping lifts 10mm Hempex
The outer ends of the twin topping lifts passed through 'D'
cleats on each side of the boom some 8ft from the outer end so
that the end of the gaff lay between two topping lifts when
lowered. Thus the topping lifts acted as 'lazy Jacks'. Each was
led up to a bull's-eye set into a strop passed round the mast at
the hounds, and each fall having a single block spliced into its
end. A further length of 10mm Hempex was led from the pin

rail on the shrouds through the block, the fall returning to the same belaying pin facilitating a 2 to 1 purchase. In practice the topping lifts may be set up at the beginning of the season and not require further adjustment.

Topsail halyard 10mm Hempex
The tops'l halyard was a single whip led from the deck through a block on the aft side of the mast shackled to the cap bend, and back to the deck. Both fall and standing parts were arranged to be the same side of the gaff and boom.

Topsail sheet 10mm Hempex
The tops'l sheet was led from the deck outside the topping lift on the same side of the boom and gaff as the topsail halyard, through a bull's-eye set in a lizard at the outer end of the gaff, back between the gaff and same topping lift, through a bull's-eye set in a lizard at the throat, and back to the deck.

When the sail is set, the sheet then runs from the clew, to the outer end of the gaff, along the gaff and to the deck. It is important to note that when sending the sail aloft outside of the topping lift (ie not between the topping lift and the mainsail) the standing part of the sheet is also outside of the topping lift to prevent the sheet becoming ensnared.

Topsail downhaul 10mm Hempex
A single whip, led from tops'l tack to the fife rail.

Gantline 10mm Hempex
A single length led from the forward pin on one shroud pin rail through a block on the fore side of the mast at the truck to the same pin on the opposite side. It is used for sending gear aloft when working from the bosun's chair, and doubles up as a halyard for setting the large jib along with the Harry Driver.

Jib halyard 10mm Hempex tackle
A 2:1 arrangement, the top block set on to a strop passed around the mast at the cap.

Staysail halyard 10mm Hempex
Single whip, led from the deck through a single block at the hounds set on to a strop passed around the mast, and back to the deck.

Jib outhaul 10mm Hempex
From a traveller the outhaul is led through a sheave set into the bowsprit at its outer end, back to the heel of the bowsprit and thence to the traveller. (At the heel of the bowsprit there is a cleat to enable the outhaul to be made fast.)

Bobstay ¼in galvanised chain. 2:1 purchase tackle. Double whip at the tackle fall.
The double block of the tackle was shackled to the outer end of the bowsprit; the chain was shackled to the single block on the tackle and to the fitting on the forefoot. The fall of the tackle had a single block spliced into its end. From a cleat on the heel of the bowsprit a whip was led through this block and back to the cleat. The arrangement gives a 6:1 purchase on the bobstay.

Jib and staysail sheets 12mm Hempex
All the jib and stays'l sheets are single whips led through fairleads on the foredeck to cleats on the side decks either side of the cockpit. (There are no sheet winches.)

General note
On the running rigging all splices were served, and on all rope ends sail makers' whippings were used.
  Matthew Walker stopper knots were used on the ends of the topping lifts (both standing part and purchase falls), the mainsheet ends and the bobstay final purchase fall. All the halyards were left whipped to allow removal from their respective blocks to facilitate maintenance.

APPENDIX 4
TOOLS

The occasional reference to tools has been made in the text but it is a subject which requires specific attention. Since the use of tools is wide and intensely personal, only the tools used during the restoration of the *Janet* will be mentioned, with comments on the odd items which may have made life easier. Illus 38.

There are the traditional shipwrights' and boat-builders' tools which although hard to find are essential for undertaking such work. A typical example is an adze; it is quite feasible to use a modern cast-steel body plane in place of a traditional box-wood plane, but there is no substitute for an adze. Another example is caulking irons and mallet, incidentally still reasonably easily obtainable from established chandlers. A substitute mallet can be used, but the balance and satisfying, if ear shattering, ring will be lost. For decorative work such as beads and forms on the edges of tables, hatches and planks, just following what was done by the bygone shipwright and using what is available and not attempting the ridiculous will still produce pleasing results.

Whatever is being used, never think that it will be quicker to continue with a blunt tool. It never is, and usually results in a bad piece of workmanship or damage to the tool or person using it. Without exception, a better and quicker job will be the result if time is taken to maintain razor-sharp edges on all cutting tools. Not only edges but correct and firm sets on saws should also be maintained at all times. This applies to power tools as much if not more so to hand tools, since there is a limit to the effort humans are prepared to exert, whereas an electric motor is likely to be damaged if it is run continuously overloaded. A blunt cutting edge requires more effort to push it through timber forming a chip than does a sharp tool. The electric power tools used were few and basic but invaluable. It is probably not advisable to try to get away with fewer than those mentioned below, particularly in these days of very cheap DIY supermarkets.

ELECTRIC TOOLS

The **10in circular saw**, hand held, did all the major sawing work such as the tapers on the deck and hull planks, but since a saw bench was not at hand and expensive to buy, timber was ordered from the sawmills largely cut to size. A reasonably powerful saw bench would have been very useful, but not imperative.

A **½in chuck Wolf drill** was the true workhorse of the rebuild and could not have been omitted sensibly from the tool chest. In fact two power drills would be advantageous since screw or spike holes usually need two sizes of hole bored. For a rebuild of a vessel comparable to the size of the *Janet* a smaller power drill would not really be powerful enough.

The **4in electric planer** was an essential part of the tool chest and saved much time and effort. Again, in these days of cheap electrical gear this is a must. Always purchase the sort that has blades that can be sharpened since working with hard wood soon dulls an edge and disposable blades would prove more expensive after a time, even if the initial cost was higher.

Other than a cheap **jig saw** which was useful for light work, those were the only power tools which were used, with two exceptions. When drilling the old keel bolts out of the keel, a **¾in heavy-duty drill** was borrowed, and when the iroko cabin sides were planed to ensure a smooth surface without steps the planks themselves were taken to a bench planer.

Certainly a wide range of power tools would have saved time and effort but were by no means necessary; their usefulness after the completion of the task would need careful appraisal before investing large sums of money in them rather than in the vessel itself.

Illus 38 Tools

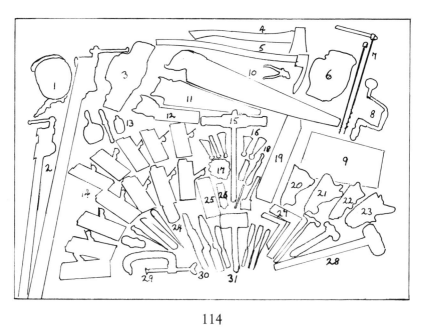

Tools

1 Pitch pot and gas ring	18 Oakum rake
2 Sash cramps	19 Boxwood jack plane 3in
3 Electric plane 4in	20 Smoothing plane 3in
4 Axe	21 Smoothing plane 2in
5 Adze	22 Rabbet plane
6 Electric saw 10in	23 Round plane
7 Augers	24 Sailmaker's palm
8 Brace	Tulip spike
9 Set of augers	Rigging knife
10 Cross-cut saw 38in	Lignum vitae fid
11 Rip saw 24in	25 Oil stone
12 Tenon saw 10in ·	26 Rule, pencil, marking gauge
13 Double and single blocks	27 Square and bevel
and belaying pin	28 7lb hammer 'Bill Scott'
14 Set of bead planes	2lb and 8oz hammers
15 Caulking mallet	29 'G' cramp 6in
16 Caulking irons	30 Boxwood spoke shave
17 Hand of oakum	31 Chisels and mallet

Hand tools are in a different category and there are many that one cannot successfully do without.

ADZE

Dating back to pre-Noah days, there are now several types of adze. The shipwright's adze has a narrow hammer head or pein on its heel, which enables any fastenings encountered to be driven below the surface of the timber being worked. For any boat work similar to the rebuild of the *Janet* it is an essential implement. It is possible to remove substantial amounts of timber very quickly and efficiently, and leave a surface which is smooth and requiring only a light plane to finish.

Learning to use an adze requires patience and practice. When working on a baulk, it is customary to stand astride the timber, hold the top of the helve firmly into the groin and work with a swinging motion with the other hand, holding the trunk stooping forward rigidly. It is imperative to maintain a razor-sharp edge on the adze at all times since a blunt edge will tend to bounce off the surface with the risk of embedding the blade in the lower part of one's leg or ankle. Any other position for adzing is a variation on this basis, whether it is level with one's midrift working on a vertical plane or, in exceptional circumstances, overhead. The idea is the same – the top of the helve is held firmly and still, while the effort is applied with the other hand held conveniently half-way down. It will probably be found when buying a new tool that the helve will need to be cut down to suit the user, and possibly the cutting edge ground back to give the blade more thickness and a chisel edge, so that the chip tends to be broken off rather than the blade becoming embedded in the timber. Finally, it will soon be discovered that the adze will perform duties that no other tool can sensibly do; for example, cutting the concave shape into the garboards of the *Janet*.

CHISELS

There is not much one can say about chisels other than as with all tools it is important to purchase those of good quality. They will retain their cutting edge for longer, and it will be possible to have a sharper edge on a harder tool steel than on a softer metal. The chisels used for the rebuild of the *Janet* were **Marples chisels** and ranged from 1 ½in down to ¼in in ¼in stages. For some reason the 1in was the handiest; but in the course of the work, all the sizes were necessary.

Bevelled chisels will cut better than those with a square back. Never sharpen the blade from the wrong side; if that is done it will not cut. The 'wire' which is left after honing can be 'stropped' off using the palm of one's hand.

Finally, always use a wooden mallet to strike a chisel, even those with plastic or composition handles. The palm of one's hand will for ever be thankful that a hammer is never used so that the top of the handle remains smooth and round.

PLANES

A variety of planes is essential and those used on the *Janet* were: **18in (long) 3in boxwood jack plane; 3in and 2in smoothing**

plane; 2in round plane; 1½in rebate plane, and various **bead** and **profile planes** all made from boxwood and used for decoration.

Each plane has its own particular merits, and experience will soon dictate which is the most handy for each job. Many times a router would render the rebate plane redundant, but not always, and certainly when joining, the rebate plane is essential. The round plane has a spring steel shoe into which the blade is set and by turning a thumb screw the shoe can be changed from being convex through to concave – invaluable when smoothing off the undersides of deck beams or planing hollow edges on to planks.

The bead planes were luckily bought from a newspaper advertisement. The set comprises beads from ¾in to ⅛in in ⅛in steps. The forming planes in my possession will do everything from picture rails to church pews! It is sad to note that various antique dealers are regarding boxwood bead and forming planes as curios, which inflates their price beyond reason. There are, however, still a few available from second-hand chandleries. To add decoration to the various structural parts of the vessel as work proceeds will maintain its period character.

As with chisels, never sharpen a plane blade from the wrong side or the result will be the same – it just will not cut.

SAWS

As with planes, a variety of saws is necessary, each to do its work at the appropriate time. The magnificent **forged-steel-blade rip saw** which proved invaluable when cutting baulks of timber has already been mentioned, but the others included **30in** and **24in rip saws, 15in** and **10in tenon saws** and a **keyhole saw.** Sensibly this proved to be as few as one could 'get away' with, but at the same time a most efficient range. For the joinery below, the two sizes of tenon saw were essential.

These days it is possible to purchase saws which 'never need sharpening'! It would be a mistake to believe this and acquire that sort. When renovating an old vessel it is quite likely that one will hit an old and obscured fastening with a saw which will damage the most prestigious cutting edge. It may be possible to resharpen after a fashion the 'never sharpen'-type blade, but the material from which it is made will prove too brittle to reset, and the saw will very quickly become useless.

It is necessary to have a **saw tooth setting tool**. After about two sharpenings the set of each tooth will tend to be lost. If one looks at a new saw sighting along the line of the teeth, each tooth is set one way and the next tooth the other. This is so the groove cut in the timber is slightly wider than the thickness of the material from which the saw blade is made, thus preventing the saw from becoming nipped in the cut. Even so it has been found that by rubbing candle wax over the sides of the saw blade the effort required to make the cut is greatly reduced. Incidentally, the same tip can be applied to a cast-steel-bodied plane. By waxing the base, the effort required to slide the plane over the wood is reduced. Boxwood planes of course are self-lubricating and do not require waxing.

The saw set is a hand-operated tool which will reset the teeth readily and accurately. A saw which is not precisely set will tend to wander off when cutting through a thick piece of timber, even to the extent of becoming jammed in the cut. Saws set with pliers will often do this.

Maintaining saws well will result in more accurate cutting and confidence in one's own skills; accurate first-time cutting will always produce a better job and save many hours of whittling down to size.

DRILLS

Drills are important, and included in the tool chest were a **brace** and **augurs** ranging from 1in to ¼in in ⅛in steps, a **belly brace, two hand drills** and **drill bits**, and **counter bores** and **counter sinks** in abundance. One can never have too many. Also a range of **dowel cutters** is a must, since any external fastening must be covered by a dowel of the correct size, and to obtain a decent finish below, fastenings need to be covered.

Dowels need to be made of the same material as the wood into which they are inserted, and the grain run the same way. This sounds obvious, but some modern vessels will display a multitude of contrasting dowels placed at extraordinary angles. Well-placed dowels will soon blend into the parent timber and disappear. The reason for mentioning dowels along with drills is that to make dowels sharp cutters should be used in a power drill, mounted on a stand to ensure no twisting or lateral movement occurs.

Finally, the more drills one has the better, since it is easier when working with two sizes of hole, and a dowel hole to drill for each fastening, just to pick up a ready-loaded tool than to keep changing bits. It is possible to buy a bit which will drill the three sizes in one, but they always seem to be the wrong combination, or wring off in a seasoned oak. The latter can be very frustrating.

HAMMERS

Even hammers and mallets can be quite an involved subject. As always, the correct hammer will make life easier. The range used on the *Janet* rebuild were a **7lb sledge hammer** with a short shaft, known affectionately as 'Bill Scott' after one of its owners in times past, through to a **4lb** and **2lb ball-pein hammer** down to an **8oz tack hammer**. The 2lb ball-pein hammer was the mainstay of the work. A claw hammer was not favoured as being too light as a hammer, and less useful than a proper 'gemmy'.

The only adage which comes to mind concerning hammers is that 'one sharp blow with a stout hammer will do less harm and be more use than a myriad of half-hearted taps'.

MEASURING INSTRUMENTS

Measuring instruments are of paramount importance, and good-quality equipment will more than repay extra cost in saved time, timber and temper. Used during the work were

100ft steel tape, 10ft steel tape and a **3ft folding boxwood scale.** Among others were **calipers** and a **depth gauge, 9in adjustable square,** two **carpenter's bevels,** a **6in vernier calliper** for engineering work, and a **boxwood metre rule** provided a usable straight edge. The best straight edge would have been a piece of **1½in aluminium angle iron** cut to the required length. However, the metre rule sufficed. Bear in mind it is much quicker to measure twice and cut once! Often a quick sketch on the piece of wood in question or in a notebook will very often clarify a slightly hesitant thought.

Always buy bevels in pairs since often when fitting, a combination of angles will be encountered and to be able to check readily two angles without recourse to resetting bevels at every turn will speed up the work and prevent errors.

CLAMPS

When boat building one can never have enough clamps. When laminating forms (fortunately when dealing with traditional work this seldom occurs) literally hundreds of clamps are required. For the *Janet* one **12in,** one **10in,** two **6in** and two **3in 'G' clamps** were used together with two **6ft sash clamps.** Although these sufficed, they were really not enough. If it had been possible, four more 6in and two more 12in 'G' clamps would have made life easier but it is surprising what can be done with wedges and shores.

CAULKING IRONS

Caulking irons are still obtainable from good chandlers', and those together with a caulking mallet will ensure good seams, not over-caulked. The distinctive mallets are usually made of lignum vitae but the lighter types can be made from boxwood. The latter is perfectly adequate for yacht work or cabin tops, etc on larger vessels. The types of irons are many and varied but fall into two main ones. The knife is used to lay initially the thread into the seam, and the tamping iron is then used to harden or tamp it down. The groove on the bottom of the tamping iron is to form a central ridge on the oakum, allowing the marine glue or the paying up material to key on to it firmly, as well as the plank edges forming a good watertight joint. (Illus 22.)

Always use the correct thickness of iron for the seam; too narrow will leave oakum up the sides of the planks causing a leak through the paying up material, and too wide will bruise the plank edges and may jam the iron preventing the proper hardening down of the oakum. The larger tamping irons have two grooves on the bottom and will be required for hardening caulking on larger vessels.

One most important item for the tool chest is a very good **oil stone**. It is worth becoming proficient in sharpening chisels and plane blades by hand without recourse to a honing guide. By keeping the wrists rigid while honing a blade will ensure the angle is maintained. Feel dictates a lot and practice (there will be plenty) will soon result in speedy and efficient sharpening. Using a honing guide will not be as quick or give such good results as will be achieved once the art has been learnt.

The remainder of the chest was made up from a wide range of tools. Their number included pincers and pliers, socket and open-ended spanners, screwdrivers, punches, centre punches, dollies for backing rivets, an anvil which was extremely handy, scribers and pencils, notepads and clipboards, compasses and dividers, a selection of files, hacksaws and other metal-working tools, and of course a stout bench and vice.

It is worth spending some time fitting out a workshop with all the tools readily to hand. Shadow boards hung around the walls proved invaluable. It was possible just to reach for the desired tool without even looking after a few weeks, and anything missing or left out after a day's work showed up instantly.

Finally the adage, 'a poor workman always blames his tools', although a good pointer is not wholly correct since poor tools will not produce as fine a job as good-quality tools in the same pair of hands. Certainly, penny pinching on tools will prove more expensive in the long run.

121

GLOSSARY OF TERMS

Adze The principal tool of the old ship builder. It resembles a garden mattock but with a longer and sharper blade curved inwards towards the helve.

Aft, Abaft or (After) At or towards the stern of a ship; in the rear. Backward motion.

Aloft Above, overhead, anywhere about the yards, masts and rigging of ships.

Apron A strong piece of timber fitted on the inner side of the stem to which it is bolted. It may be composed of more than one piece of timber.

Backstay A stay run from the top part of the mast and led to a chain plate well abaft the mast preventing the mast bending forward and sideways.

Baggywrinkle A home-made substance made out of old rope to prevent the sails chafing on lifts, stays, or any part of the ship's rigging. In the case of the text, the author's St Bernard.

Ballast Additional weight carried in the ship to give her stability and/or to provide a satisfactory trim.

Ballast keel The keel of a yacht shaped to suit the underwater profile of the yacht and carried externally. Its effect is that of ballast.

Baulk A sizeable piece of timber, roughly hewn from the log into a square section and often used as a temporary support for heavy pieces of machinery or boats when ashore.

Bawley A small coastal fishing vessel peculiar to Rochester and Whitstable, Kent, and to Leigh-on-Sea and Harwich, Essex, within the Thames estuary area.

Bead The decoration formed on the edge of a plank using a suitable forming plane. It is used on the underside of deck planks, beamshelves and clamps, and deck beams particularly.

Beam One of the transverse members of a ship's frames on which the decks are laid. **Halfbeam** A beam not extending from side to side of a ship, for instance, as fitted between a vessel's side and hatchway.

Beamshelf A heavy piece of timber fitted longitudinally round the side of the ship on which the deck beams rest and are fastened.

Bearing shell Usually a steel-backed piece of white metal formed to fit between the outer surface and the inner surface of a bearing, such as that found in the big ends of internal combustion engines, thus forming a bearing surface between the crankpin and the piston connecting rod.

Belay, to The operation of making fast a rope by taking turns with it round a cleat or belaying pin.

Belaying pin Short lengths of wood, iron, or brass set in racks or rails in convenient places in a ship, around which the running rigging can be secured.

Bilge The interior of the bottom of a vessel.

Bilge, turn of The turn or transition from the flat of the bottom to the upward-rising sides of a vessel.

Bitts Timbers extending vertically above a ship's deck. They are used as the strong points on a vessel for either mooring lines or towing hawsers. On smaller vessels the anchor chain is usually made fast to the bitts on the foredeck.

Block A wooden or metal case into which one or more sheaves are fitted through which a rope is passed enabling the rope to run freely.

Bobstay A chain or heavy wire running from the outer end of the bowsprit to the ship's stem or cutwater. It transmits the upward pull on the bowsprit back into the hull.

Bolt rope The name given to the rope which is sewn round the edges of a sail to carry the tension which would otherwise be found in the edge of the canvas.

Bone in her teeth The white feather of water under the bow of a ship when she is under way, usually when moving fast.

Boom The spar used on the foot of the sail extending from the

123

tack to the clew.

Bowsprit A spar of relative considerable size projecting over the fore end of a vessel, enabling jibs and staysails to be carried outboard of the stem head.

Breasthook A piece of timber across the apron of a vessel joining the two sides of the vessel together at the bow.

Bulkhead The partitions by which the below-decks compartments of a vessel are separated.

Bull's-eye A circular or elliptical piece of hardwood, often lignum vitae, which is inserted into the end of a lizard in the place of a block. It has a hole through its centre through which a rope, halyard, or sheet may pass and run freely.

Butt The flat end of a plank. The cranny between the ends of two abutting planks.

Button or Truck A circular flat piece of wood resembling a clothing button fastened to the top of a mast, its primary function is to prevent rain water running down the end grain of the timber from which the mast is made.

Cable 608ft or one-tenth of a nautical mile.

Caprail or Capping A strip of wood fitted to the top of the gunwale or round the top of the coamings in a yacht.

Carling A piece of wood fitted fore and aft between the deck beams to which hatch or cabin coamings are usually fastened.

Caulking The filling of the seams between the wooden planks with oakum or similar material.

Chain plates Strips of iron or bronze bolted to the sides of a vessel either through a frame or fitted with a backing piece to which the lower end of the shrouds or backstays is secured.

Cheek or Hound pieces Knee-shaped pieces of wood fitted either side of the mast at the hounds which carry the trestletrees and the eyes in the end of the shrouds.

Clamp A second strake of inside planking directly under the beamshelf. Supports the beamshelf and increases the strength of the gunwale of the vessel.

Cleat A piece of wood or metal with two horns placed in convenient places on vessels to enable ropes or sheets etc to be made fast.

Clench or Clinch   A simple method of fastening the hull planks to the ribs of a vessel, usually with copper nails driven right through the plank and rib with the end then hooked and turned back into the rib. A dolly is placed on the head of the nail and the end is hammered up forming a rivet.

Clew   The corner of a sail to which the sheet attaches. It is at the junction of the foot and the leech of the sail.

Close-hauled   The condition of a sailing vessel with her sails trimmed so that she may move efficiently in a direction whose bearing is as small as possible between itself and the direction from which the wind is blowing.

Coach roof   The name by which the cabin top of older yachts is known.

Coaming   The framing or raised borders round hatchways, skylight openings, etc, fastened either to carlings if longitudinal or deck beams if transverse.

Counter   The arch forming the overhanging stern of a vessel above the water-line. The term is also used to indicate the small area of deck abaft the stern post and rudder trunk.

Covering board   Usually the edge-most piece of wood of a deck covering up the top edge of the sheerstrake and the timber heads.

Crankcase   The box formed by the sump or bedplate of an engine and the skirts of the cylinder block, housing the crankshaft and connecting rods.

Crankpin   The bearing pin onto which the connecting rods are fitted.

Crankshaft   The cranked shaft to which the piston connecting rods are connected and by means of which the power generated in the cylinders of an engine is transmitted to the propeller shaft.

Crans iron   The iron band at the outer end of a bowsprit to which a jib boom is fastened if there is one or, in the case of a smaller vessel, to which the outer stay, the bobstay and the tack of the foremast jib are connected.

Cringle   A short piece of rope worked grommet-fashion into the bolt rope of a sail containing a metal thimble. In modern sails cringles are often merely punched into the material thereby reducing labour and cost.

Cutter Although in the past a cutter has referred to various types of smaller sailing ships, it currently refers to the rig of a fore-and-aft vessel having a staysail and a jib as the basic canvas forward of the main mast. These vessels carry only one mast.

Cylinder The barrel in which the piston of a reciprocating engine or pump moves backwards and forwards.

Cylinder liner A removable barrel set in the casting of an engine or pump forming the cylinder.

Dead eye A flat circular piece of wood set into the lower end of a shroud or stay, through which holes are drilled and faired so that a lanyard when passed through the holes may be used as a purchase to tighten the shroud.

Deadlight The metal covering for a porthole or in the case of the text non-opening portholes.

Deadwood Blocks of timber used as filling pieces and fitted against the stern post on the after end of the keel, and on the inner side of the stem upon the fore end of the keel on top of which they are bolted.

Dolly A weight held on the head of a nail so that the other end may be rivetted without fear of the nail being driven back out of its hole.

Dovetail The type of joint used to join the two edges of a coaming cut in such a manner that the inner edge is wider than the outer edge, so that when the joint is slid together it locks in a similar fashion to a jigsaw piece.

Dovetail, half A joint where one side is set at an angle which locks the two pieces of wood together, and the other side is straight.

Dowel A small cylindrical piece of wood used to cover the sunken head of a fastening.

Downhaul A single whip or tackle used to exert a downward force on, for example, the tack of staysail or jib.

Draught The exact depth of water required to float the vessel completely.

Entry The form of the fore body of a ship below the water-line. A ship with a slim bow is said to have a fine entry.

Eye   A soft eye is a loop in a rope or wire not having a thimble. A hard eye is a loop with a thimble tightly worked into it.

Eye-bolt   A bolt having a ring instead of a hexagonal head.

Eye splice   A loop made in the end of a wire or rope by using the strands woven into the standing part of the wire or rope.

Fairlead   An eye of a very hard wood such as lignum vitae attached to some part of the vessel to lead a rope or sheet etc in the desired direction.

Fall   The handling part of a halyard or tackle.

Fashion piece   The after-most timbers of a ship carved out of solid timber to form the actual shape of the stern where fabrication is impractical such as in the after end of the counter of a small vessel.

Fastening   The general term used to describe bolts, nails, rivets, treenails or any other fashion by means of which the component parts of a vessel are joined together.

Fid   A long tapering piece of hard material (lignum vitae or bone) used for separating the strands of a rope so that the unlaid end of it may be passed through the opening when making a splice.

Fife rail   The rail usually round three sides of the bottom of the mast carrying belaying pins to which the halyards or downhauls are made fast.

Floor   Floors are the lowest part of the various pieces of timber of which the square body frames are constructed and cross the inside of the keel.

Forecastle or Fo'c's'le   The foremost compartment of the ship in which the crew in larger vessels traditionally had their quarters.

Forefoot   The external point at which a reasonably vertical stem meets the keel. A vessel with a spoon bow is said not to have a forefoot.

Forestay   The stay from the stem head to the hounds of the foremost mast.

Fore triangle   The triangle formed ahead of the mast by the outer most or top mast forestay, the mast itself, the centre line of the foredeck and bowsprit if fitted.

Frame   One of the numerous transverse ribs that form the skeleton of the vessel.

Freeboard   The distance from the water's edge on the outside of the vessel to the top of the deck at the half length of the ship.

Fuel injector pump   The high-pressure pump on a diesel engine which supplies a precisely measured quantity of fuel to the injector at the correct moment during the engine cycle.

Fuel valve (injector)   Valve mounted in the cylinder head of a diesel engine which atomises the fuel delivered to it by the fuel injector pump.

Gaff   A spar having usually at one end a jaw partially clasping the round of a mast and to which the head rope of a trapezoidal (gaff) sail is attached.

Gammoning iron   The band may be bronze or iron fastened to the stem head of a vessel either to the side or on top through which the bowsprit passes. Originally it was a lashing made fast to the beak of seventeenth- and eighteenth-century vessels.

Gantline   Single whip passing to and from the deck through a block at the masthead which is used for sending light loads to any part of the mast.

Garboard   The bottom-most plank of the vessel running alongside and rebated into the keel. Usually somewhat thicker than the rest of the hull planks.

Genoa   A large jib or foresail which in the case of the *Janet* extends from the masthead to the bowsprit end and back to the shrouds. The size of this sail relative to the vessel is a good example of a genoa jib.

Gybe   Usually refers to fore-and-aft sails only and is the act of moving the sail from one side to the other when the wind is coming directly astern. Clearly an uncontrolled gybe in strong weather may well damage the sail, spars or rigging.

Halyard   A rope by which either a yard, gaff, sail or flag, etc is hoisted aloft.

Handy billy   The name given to a small 2:1 purchase tackle kept to hand for a variety of purposes aboard.

Harry Driver   The author's own slang for *Janet*'s light-weather genoa jib.

Head of sail The top-most point of a triangular sail; the junction between the luff and the leech.

Heads Slang for marine lavatory.

Helm Another name for the tiller, by which the rudder of small vessels, such as yachts, is swung, and also the general term associated with orders connected with the steering of a ship.

Helve The handle of an adze.

Highfield lever A form of hand-operated 'over centre' lever used aboard sailing yachts as a rapid method of setting up or tautening running backstays or forestays.

Hog or Sole piece The term used to describe the equivalent of a kelson in smaller vessels. It is the piece of wood which forms the internal backbone on which the stern post and stem are set up and under which the ballast keel is hung.

Hog, to Refers to a bend in the keel of a vessel so that the ends of the vessel are found to be in a lower horizontal plane than its centre.

Hood ends The ends of those planks in the hull structure of a wooden vessel which fit into the rabbets of the stem and stern post.

Horn timbers The fore-and-aft stern timbers running up and back from the stern post through to the extreme after end forming the backbone of the counter.

Hounds That portion of a mast upon which the trestle-trees are lodged and by which they are kept in the desired position.

Hull The bare shell of the vessel consisting of the upper deck, sides and the bottom.

Jaws (Gaff jaws) The crutch of a hollowed semi-circular projection on the inner end of a boom or gaff, loosely clasping a mast so as to permit such boom or gaff being raised or lowered on the mast.

Jib When rigged on a cutter the jib is the outer-most sail set on the bowsprit.

Joggle The shape cut into the king plank or covering board to enable the abutting deck plank to have a tapering but flat end, thus avoiding a feathered edge which tends to split when the seams are caulked.

Keel   The so-called backbone of a vessel found externally.

Keel bolt   The main bolts passing through the keel floors and kelson on a working vessel and the ballast keel, hog and floors in the case of a yacht.

Ketch   Now generally understood to be a vessel having two masts, the fore being the main mast and the mizzen stepped forward of the stern post.

King plank   The centre-most plank laid fore and aft on the deck.

Knee, hanging   Strengthening pieces formed to hang beneath the extreme ends of the beams in such a manner that they are bolted to the beam and to the beamshelf and the clamp. They are formed from suitable timber so that the grain sweeps round the knee and on the one face is parallel to the beam and on the other face is parallel to the ship's side.

Knee, lodging   A strengthening piece similarly fabricated as the hanging knee and lodged in a horizontal plane forming a stiffener between the side of the beam and the inner surface of the outer hull planking above the beamshelf.

Knightheads   The foremost frame timbers in a ship, one being placed on each side of the stem and in many working vessels extending above it to carry the transverse load from the bowsprit.

Lazy Jacks   Light pieces of rope bent into the topping lifts from a boom and passing loosely down and made fast onto the boom. Used in conjunction with twin topping lifts, their function is to gather the folds of the fore-and-aft sail when it is lowered and prevent the bulk of the canvas sliding off the boom onto the deck.

Leech   The after side or trailing side of a fore and aft sail; the edge of the sail which lies between the head of a triangular sail or the peak of a gaff sail and their respective clews.

Lines   Refers to the line plan of the vessel and normally consists of three views. The sheer plan which shows the longitudinal vertical section of the ship; the body plan which shows the vertical cross sections; and the half breadth plan which shows the longitudinal transverse section. (Illus 37.)

Lizard   A short length of rope with a thimble spliced into the end of it.

LOA   Length overall.

Luff (of sail)   The leading edge of a fore-and-aft sail, the edge that lies between the head and tack on a triangular sail, or the throat and tack on a gaff sail.

LWL   Length along water-line. The fore-and-aft length of the water-line.

Mainbearing   The bearing on the crankshaft of an engine contained by the crankcase or bedplate. The crankshaft rotates about the centre line drawn through the line of mainbearings.

Mainsail (mains'l)   The sail designated as the principal sail on the vessel. Up until recently, it was the largest fore-and-aft sail of the rig, but with the advent of high aspect ratio rigs, genoa jibs and various types of spinnaker this is no longer always true.

Marine glue   Patent preparation made from pitch resins and spirits and used to fill and waterproof seams between planks, either deck or hull, after they have been caulked. To fill the seam in this manner is called paying up a seam.

Marline   A small light twine spun from two strands. Can be tarred or untarred.

Mast   Vertical or slightly raked pole set up in a ship.

Mast band   Band of iron or bronze tightly fitted around the mast to carry blocks, shrouds, stays, etc.

Mast gaiter   A piece of canvas sewn round the mast and bound tightly to it, and fastened to the deck to form a watertight seal between the deck and the mast.

Mast partners   Horizontal pieces of wood set into the deck beams immediately below the deck planks through which the mast passes.

Mast, pole   Mast made from a single piece of timber, ie having no top mast.

Mast, step   The mortice cut into the sole piece or hog to receive the tenon cut into the keel of the mast.

Mast, top   Second mast set up above the lower or main mast. Facilitates ease of construction for larger spars, and the lowering and reduction of top weight during heavy weather.

Matthew Walker Particular kind of stopper knot.

Mavis Clark A marvellously seasoned, benign and accommodating English whore residing in Amsterdam.

Megga An ohm meter, or instrument for measuring electrical resistance.

Montagu Whaler 27ft open, double-ended, clinker-built boat peculiar to the Royal Navy. Sailed with a dipping lug or rowed, it served as a 'boat' for the RN from the mid-eighteenth century to well after World War II when, although the shape was retained, instead of being clinker built it was made from Double Diagonal strake and finally GRP.

Moulded breadth The breadth from outside to outside of the frames, ie exclusive of the thickness of the hull planking.

Moulded depth The depth measured from the top of the keel (or hog) to the top of the upper deck beam, less the 'round of the beam' or camber.

Navel pipe The pipe down which the anchor chain passes to the chain locker.

Parcel The act of wrapping canvas round a rope or wire after it has been wormed, and prior to serving, to prevent chafe or attack from the elements.

Peak (of gaff sail) The uppermost point of the sail. The junction between the head and the leech.

Pin rail Rails fitted inside the bulwarks or on the shrouds carrying belaying pins.

Pintle Metal pins fitted onto a rudder by means of straps forming a hinge pin about which the rudder turns.

Piston The linearly moving part of an internal combustion engine, arranged to fit neatly within the bore of the cylinder so that it may slide freely, and connected to the crankshaft by means of the connecting rod. Made usually from an aluminium alloy, a seal between the cylinder walls and the piston is affected by fitting hoop-shaped rings around the piston.

Piston rings Hoop seals fitted around the piston.

Planking, deck Fore-and-aft boards placed over the deck beams forming the outer skin of the deck itself.

Planking, hull Fore-and-aft boards run around the outside of the frames forming the outer skin of the vessel.

Propeller shaft   Shaft which couples to the engine at its inner end and passes through the hull via a suitable tube and gland arrangement, and carries the propeller at its outer end.

Quarter   The sides of the after end of a vessel.

Rabbet   From the word rebate. A suitable recess cut into a timber so that an adjoining piece may be 'let in' and fastened to it.

Reach   A sailing vessel is reaching when the wind is directly from over her beam. Often the fastest point of sailing.

Reef, to   The act of shortening or reducing sail to prevent damage during a wind which is too strong for a full sail.

Reef point   A short length of line sewn through the sail so that, after the ends of the sail have been pulled down to reduce its size, the ensuing bundle of spare canvas may be folded and contained by tying together the two ends of each reef point in a reef knot.

Rib   As for frame, but whereas a frame will be made from suitably shaped grown or compass timber the rib, although having the same function as a frame, will be steamed to shape and very much lighter than a piece of shaped timber. Generally a yacht will have ribs, and a working vessel will be built with frames.

Rigging   General name given to all the wire, chain or rope aloft.

Rigging, running   Refers to all halyards, sheets, downhauls, etc which are not fixed.

Rigging, standing   The shrouds, stays, backstays, etc which are all fixed.

Rigging screw   A bottle screw or tensioning device for wire. When the centre portion is turned, the two outer ends having opposing threads either close in or lengthen depending upon the rotation. Used as an in-line tensioner for shrouds and stays.

Rudder stock   A bar (either iron or timber) rising up from the fore side of the rudder by means of which the rudder is controlled. In the case of a balanced rudder the stock is joined to the rudder aft of its leading edge.

Run (before the wind)   A vessel sailing with the wind coming from directly astern. Very uncomfortable in a fore-and-aft-rigged vessel owing to the ever present danger of a gybe.

Run (of ship)   The narrowing of the vessel's bottom from the belly to the stern post. A vessel having a fine run will leave the water with less fuss than a vessel with a short full run and bulbous quarters when passing through it.

Running backstay   A temporary stay led from the masthead of a yacht to the windward rail abaft the beam and tensioned with a tackle or highfield lever. The leeward backstay if left rigged would foul the boom so it is cast off and belayed at the main shrouds. When the yacht adopts the other tack, the leeward backstay becomes the windward and is set as the vessel passes through the wind while the windward backstay becomes the leeward and is let off.

Samson post   The post set up on the fore deadwoods and passing through the deck, secured to a deck beam, to carry the heel of the bowsprit and to act as a mooring bitt.

Scantlings   The dimensions of the individual components from which the hull and deck of a vessel are constructed.

Scarf   The joint between two pieces of timber with the same cross-sectional dimensions, so that the one tapers into the other, the cross-sectional dimensions remaining the same.

Seam   The gaps between the sides of the planks from which the vessel is built.

Serve   To bind a rope or wire tightly with spun yarn after it has been wormed and parcelled using a serving mallet to achieve as much tension as possible in the spun yarn. The seaman's ditty to do each action correctly is as follows: 'Worm and parcel with the lay, turn and serve the other way.'

Shaft log   The outermost bearing on the propeller shaft, usually rubber or lignum vitae, contained in a bronze carrier which bolts onto the after edge of the stern post, or is supported by an A bracket in the case of a wing engine. The bearing is water-lubricated.

Shake   A longitudinal crack running along the grain of a piece of timber caused by drying out. It is not detrimental to the strength of a spar, provided there are not too many and they at no time run across the grain.

Sheerlegs   Two poles, set up in an inverted 'V' with a lifting tackle fastened to the apex to facilitate the lifting of a heavy object. The sheerlegs lean slightly from the vertical, and are controlled by a guy rope from the apex.

Sheer line   The upward curve of the deck of a vessel from the lowest part of the deck up to the bow and stern.

Sheerstrake   The topmost of the hull planks.

Sheet   The rope by means of which the sail is trimmed to the wind or controlled.

Shipwright   The tradesman whose craft encompasses the structural part of wooden ship building. He is distinct from a boat builder but obviously there is a certain amount of overlap. Originally a master shipwright would build a ship by eye from a half model without recourse to drawings.

Shore   A prop to prevent a vessel toppling when standing on her keel out of the water.

Shroud   The standing rigging on a mast or spar giving lateral support.

Sloop   A vessel with one mast, one jib and one fore-and-aft mainsail.

Soft eye   A loop spliced in the end of a rope or wire without a thimble or heart in the eye.

Sole   The cabin and cockpit decks on yachts.

Sole piece   See **Hog**.

Span   A rope or wire secured to the gaff by both its ends and fitted with a traveller to which a peak halyard block is rigged. Its effect is to transmit the load in the peak halyard to two points on the spar instead of one.

Spanish windlass   A continuous loop of rope pulled tightly between two points, and with a lever at the mid point. When the lever is rotated and the loop twisted, the ends of the loop are drawn together with considerable force.

Splice   The act of joining two ropes or forming an eye in the end of a single rope by weaving the unlaid strands of the end of the rope into the lay of the standing part.

Spoon bow   Type of bow found on yachts where the stem lets into the hog almost parallel to it, and bends gracefully towards the vertical at deck level. A vessel having a spoon bow has no forefoot.

Spreaders Struts fitted to the sides of a mast to enable a shroud to rise vertically from the chain plate to the spreader before closing in towards the mast higher up. The heel of the spreader will be found at the hounds, ie where the lower shroud is made fast to the mast.

Staysail The fore-and-aft triangular sail found immediately ahead of a mast, when there are further sails ahead of it.

Stem The heavy, often curving, piece of timber making the foremost part of the vessel's hull.

Stern The after-most part of a vessel's hull.

Stern gland The watertight gland through which the propeller shaft passes.

Stern post A stout piece of timber rising from the aft end of the keel into which the lower plank ends are rabbeted and from which the rudder is hung.

Stern tube The tube having the shaft log at its outer end and the stern gland at its inner end, and through which the propeller shaft passes.

Stockholm tar A resin and linseed-oil based compound used for protecting seizings on rigging from weather attack. It can also be used to prevent chickens pecking each other by application to the feathers.

Stopwater A dowel fitted across the faces of a submerged scarf (ie in the keel) to prevent water creeping up the scarf and into the bilge.

Strake A continuous run of planking or timber from end to end of the vessel.

Stringer A longitudinal timber fitted internally to increase the fore-and-aft strength of the vessel.

Stuffing box See **Stern gland**.

Tack (of sail) The lower foremost corner of a fore-and-aft sail. The junction of the luff and the foot.

Tack (of ship) A vessel is said to be on the starboard tack when she is close-hauled with the wind coming over the starboard side; conversely for the port tack.

Tack, to The act of bringing the vessel head to wind and allowing the vessel to bear away and assume a direction of sailing with the wind coming from the opposite side.

Talurit A patent method of splicing a thimble into a wire rope. The wire's end is passed through an alloy ferule, round the thimble and back through the ferule. It is pulled tight, the ferule compressed thus gripping the wire, and the fall is cut flush with the top of the ferule.

Thimble A grooved iron or bronze ring either heart-shaped or round, contained in an eye splice of wire or rope to provide a shackle point. It prevents chafe of the parent rope or wire.

Throat The top forward corner of a gaff sail. It is the junction between the head and the luff of the sail.

Tiller The lever at the top of the rudder stock by means of which the rudder is turned.

Toe rail On a yacht it is the rail which runs round the edge of the covering board just inboard of the gunwale, which acts as a foothold when the yacht is heeling and prevents objects rolling overboard.

Tongued and grooved (T & G) When two planks lie side by side, one has a groove cut down the middle of the side (lengthways) and the other has a rebate cut in the top and bottom edge of the side, thus leaving a tongue or fillet protruding so that it fits the groove exactly in the adjacent plank.

Topping lift The rope or wire which supports the outer end of a spar by running from the end of the spar, through a block higher up the mast on which the spar is located.

Topsail (tops'l) In the case of a gaff topsail, it is the sail which fills the space between the gaff and the masthead.

Topsail, jackyard A topsail laced to poles so that it may extend above the masthead and beyond the end of the gaff, but still be hoisted from the deck.

Topsides (of a yacht) The painted area between the waterline and the gunwale.

Transom The athwartship timbers bolted to the stern post of a ship to give a flat stern.

137

Traveller   The leather-bound iron or bronze ring which slides on a spar having a sail or second spar as in the case of a lugsail fastened to it.

Trestle-trees   The fore-and-aft pieces of timber which lie across the top of the hounds, preventing the shrouds from cutting into the end grain of the hounds, and extending forward to carry the topmast fid.

Truck   See **Mast cap**.

Ultra violet light   Part of the invisible spectrum emitted by the sun which tends to destroy man-made fibres such as Terylene.

Water sail   A small triangular sail hung under the boom of a gaff sail in light airs to increase the sail area for downwind work.

Weather-helm   The tendency a sailing vessel has for steering itself into the wind.

Work-harden   The phenomenon which causes metal to become harder and more brittle than originally, due to a continuously changing load and subsequent continuous bending or plastic deformation.

Worm, to   Originally cunting – the act of working a small line into the grooves between the strands of a wire rope or cable. It is done prior to parcelling and then serving.

Yard, topsail   The spar to which the gaff topsail is laced so that the head of the topsail may extend beyond the top of the mast but still be sent aloft on a halyard from the deck.

INDEX

Numbers in italics refer to illustrations

Accommodation 73, 75–9, *76*
Adze 23, 51, 65, 115, 122
Apron 18, 20, 35, 96, 122
Armour of Fleetwood 11

Backstay 80, 122
Baggywrinkle 80, 122
Ballast 82–3, 106, 122
Ballast keel 13, 46, 62, 97, 122
Barnacle 10
Bawley 24, 86, 122
Bead 42, 112, 114, 122
Beam 10, 14, 20, 34–6, 52, 56, 96, 106, 123
Beamshelf 10, 14, 18, 33, 52, 96, 106, 123
Bearing shell 101, 123
Bedding compound 48
Beeswax 53
Belaying pin 70, 123
Big class yacht 84, 87
Big end bearing 47
Bilge 33, 59, 70, 92, 123
Bilge plank 50, 104
Bitt 56, 70, 123
Block 81, 123
Bobstay 10, 56, 111, 123
Bolt rope 71, 123
Bone in her teeth 89, 123
Bones 13, 96
Boom 25, 84, 107, 123
Bosun's chair 70
Bow 83
Bowsprit 10, 25, 56, 70, 81, 107, 124
Boxwood plane 65, 112
Breasthook 18, 34, 98, 124
Bronze 97
Bulkhead 75, 124

Bulldog grip 68
Bull's-eye 82, 124
Bunk 75
Butt 29, 36, 54, 124
Button 66, 124

Cabin 25, 27, 39
Cabin side 27, 39
Camber 27
Canadian spruce 65
Carling 10, 19, 34, *37*, 39, 106, 124
Catch 68
Caulking 10, 43, 56, 57, 62, 97, 124
Caulking iron 120
Caulking mallet 43, 120
Cement 99
Chafe 100
Chain plate 81, 96, 124
Chart drawer 77
Chart table 77
Cheek 66, 124
Chisel 116
Clamp 18, 34, 106, 124
Cleat 124; *see* Mooring cleat and sheet cleat
Clench 17, 125
Clew 25, 80, 100, 125
Coach roof 27, 42, 54, 125
Coaming 9, 36, 39, 53, 93, 96, 106, 125
Cockpit 9, 25, 27, 39
Cockpit sole 57
Cooker 75
Copper 12, 97
Counter 12, 28–33, *32*, *33*, 61, 75, 97, 125
Covering board 36, *37*, 106, 125
Crane 14, 62

139

Index

Crankcase 47, 101, 125
Crankpin 101, 125
Crankshaft 47, 49, 101, 125
Crans iron 108, 125
Cringle 71, 125
Crossfield of Arneside 11
Cutlass bearing 48
Cutter 10, 84, 126
Cylinder liner 101, 126

Deadeye 68, 126
Deadlight 13, 126
Deadwood 13, 17, 18, 35, 47, 92, 96, 98, 104, 126
Deck 10, 26, 41, 58, 58, 79, 96
Deck plank 36–9, 38, 40, 60, 106
Derrick 68
Dolly 22, 126
Douglas fir 81
Dovetail 34, 126
Dowel 37, 56, 126
Downhaul 86, 110, 126
Drill 118
Drive screw 21, 23

Elm 13, 22, 30, 68
Engine 46–9, 71, 73, 92, 101
Engine bed 47, 102
Engine box 57, 77
English oak 47, 52, 53, 97
Eye bolt 66, 127
Eye slice 127; see Splice

Fairlead 59, 72, 82, 127
Fashion piece 18, 19, 30, 31, 62, 100, 127
Fastening 12, 96, 127
Fid 115, 127
Fife rail 70, 127
Floor 18, 47, 50–1, 96, 104, 127
Foc'sle 10, 75, 127
Fore deck 56
Forefoot 11, 127
Fore hatch 25, 36, 53
Forestay 56, 108, 127
Fore triangle 82, 127
Frame 33, 96, 128
Freeboard 75, 128

Fuel tank 97
Fuel valve 101, 128

Gaff 25, 81, 107, 128
Gaiter, mast 100, 131
Galley 75
Gammoning iron 10, 13, 59, 70, 128
Gantline 110, 128
Garboard 12, 17, 22–4, 23, 33, 97, 128
Garboard seam 51, 97, 99
Gaskin 57
Gear box 49, 101
Gear lever 74, 74
Genoa 82, 128
Gimbal 68, 75
Graving piece 12
Gybe 88, 128

Half beam 34, 42, 123
Halyard 66, 69, 70, 81, 89, 100, 109, 110, 128
Handy billy 48, 128
Harry Driver 82, 84, 86, 128
Hatch 42, 53, 53, 106
Head of sail 100, 129
Heads 98, 129
Headsail 25
Helve 115, 129
Highfield lever 80, 129
Hinge 53
Hog 18, 51, 96, 104, 129
Hog, to 13, 96, 129
Hood end 97, 129
Horn timbers 18, 28–31, 31, 97, 100, 104, 129
Hound 65, 68, 69, 129
Hull 17, 18, 19, 20, 26, 28, 51, 70, 95, 100, 129
Hythe Quay 60, 72

Iroko 39
Inertia 68
Inventory 102

Jaw, gaff 129
Jib 56, 71, 80, 81, 83, 86, 110, 111, 129

Joggle 36, 38, *38*, 129

Kapur 36, 51
Keel 12, 45, 96, 104, 130
Keel bolt 44–6, *45*, 97, 130
Ketch 94, 130
King plank 36, *38*, 39, 43, 130
Knee 20, 52, 96, 104, 130
Knighthead 19, 20, 35, 130
Knot (in wood) 65

Lamp 68
Larch 30, 33, 34, 42, 70, 81
Launch 59, 62–4, *63*
Lazy Jack 109, 130
Lee bow 83
Leech 80, 130
Lifting sling 62
Lignum vitae 70, 72
Lines, of Janet 105, 130
Linseed oil 17, 30, 59, 79
Lizard 82, 131
Locker 57, 75, 97
Log book 71
Luff 83, 89, 131
Luff of sail 80, 81, 131

Magnet 47, 49
Mainbearing 101
Mainsail 25, 71, 80, 86, 131
Marine glue 57, 77, 131
Marline 68, 131
Marstal engine 73
Mast 10, 24, 27, 65–9, *67*, 96, 107, 131
Mast band 66, 131
Mast partner 19, 36, 39, 100, 131
Mast splice 101
Matthew Walker 111, 132
Mavis Clark 89, 132
Megga 102, 132
Mildew 98
Montague Whaler 21, 36
Mooring cleat 59
Morecambe Bay Prawner 9–12, 25, 32, 50
Mould 98
Moulded breadth 132

Moulded depth 132
Mud berth 50

Navel pipe 132
Needle 68

Oakum 56, 57
Old Gaffers Race 80, 86–90
Outhaul 111

Paint 17, 57
Panelling 75
Parcel 108, 132
Pay-up 43, 57
Peak 66, 81, 89, 100, 109, 132
Pig iron 106
Pilot hole 44
Pin rail 132
Piston 101, 132
Piston ring 101, 132
Plane 116
Plank 11, 20, 43, 104, 132
Plans of hull and deck 26
Plumb line 33
Poop deck 36
Port hole 54–5, *55*
Propeller shaft 48, 133

Quarter sawn timber 12, *12*

Rabbet 29, *33*, 97, 133
Reach 89, 133
Rebuild 91, 94, 100
Reef point 100, 133
Renovation 94, 100
Resin 17
Rib 13, 18–22, 96, 98, 104, 133
Rigging *10*, 69, 107–11
Rigging screw 68, 133
Rot 95, 96, 98
Rudder 49–50, 92
Rudder stock 39, 50, 133
Rudder stock trunk 28
Running backstay 80, 134
Running rigging 70, 109, 133

Sailing beam 19, 27, 34
Sail loft 24

Index

Sail plan 25
Saloon 78, 79
Samson post 27, 134
Sash cramp 36, 120
Scantling 25, 94, 104–6, 105, 134
Scarf 23, 34, 36, 42, 134
Seam 36, 57, 134
Seamflex 79
Seizing 68
Serve 108
Serving 68, 134
Shaft log 48, 92, 134
Shake 12, 134
Sheer 33
Sheerleg 48, 135
Sheer line 33, 95, 135
Sheerstrake 19, 28, 33, 33, 135
Sheet 69, 80, 81, 82, 88, 89, 100, 109, 110, 135
Sheet cleat 70
Shore 14, 22, 33, 62, 135
Shroud 68, 81, 100, 108, 135
Sink 75, 97
Skylight 27, 42, 53–5, 55, 77, 106
Smell 97, 98
Soft eye 68, 135
Sole or sole piece 135; see Hog
Span 109, 135
Span shackle 68
Spar 25
Splice 70, 135
Spoon bow 11, 75, 135
Stanchion 70
Standing rigging 68–70, 100, 108
Stay 100
Staysail 71, 80, 81, 89, 111, 136
Steamer 21
Stem 11, 18, 20, 33, 96, 97, 104, 136
Stern gland 101, 136
Stern post 12, 18, 27, 48, 92, 97, 100, 104, 136
Stern tube 48, 136
Stockholm tar 68, 136
Stopping 57
Stopwater 18, 136
Stress 96, 100

Stringer 19, 51, 136
Stuffing box 48, 136
Survey 11, 93–103
Swig up 70, 81, 89

Tack 80, 88, 90, 137
Tack of sail 81, 100, 136
Talurit 68, 137
Tar 17
Tar varnish 45, 57, 59
Terylene 71, 82, 100
Thimble 68, 137
Throat 66, 100, 109, 137
Throttle 74, 74
Tie bolt 39
Tiller 13, 83, 137
Toe rail 59, 60, 137
Tongue and groove 10, 77, 137
Tools 112–21, 114
Tools, electric 113
Topping lift 69, 109, 137
Topsail 68, 81, 86, 89, 110, 137
Top shroud or cap shroud 68, 108
Topside 10, 57, 85, 137
Trailer 14, 60
Transom 28, 29, 137
Transport beams 15
Traveller 70, 138
Trestle tree 66, 138
Twine 68
Twist 96

Ultra violet light 100, 138

Varnish 17, 43, 54, 59

Water line 64
Water sail 84, 88, 89, 138
Weather-helm 24, 80–3, 138
Whipping 111
Wooden block 70, 100
Worm 108, 138
Wrought 13, 96

Yard 10, 68, 82, 107, 138
Yellow pine 12, 104

142